World's Most
ENDANGERED

World's Most
ENDANGERED

Sophie McCallum

Eastern Lowland Gorilla exhibiting tool use.

Contents

Northern Bald Ibis.

Introduction

STARING AT A MASS EXTINCTION?

As I sat in an Oxford University lecture hall a decade ago, the lecturer was professing that unless legislation was passed at a political level the Earth's climate would change irreversibly in ten years time and we would be helpless to do anything about it. Chemicals would have reacted in the atmosphere, creating permanent climate change. A decade has passed and the news reporting around the subject of the environment has adapted from hard, shock tactics about climate change, that numb people to it, to softer reporting on iconic often fluffy animals and how they are endangered. This only scratches the surface.

With the world's human population set to rise to 8.5 billion by 2030 it is hardly a surprise that we are experiencing large-scale loss, degradation and fragmentation of natural habitats, which is the key concern for the majority of species at risk of extinction. The trouble is that we have reached a point of no return. Although the human population growth rate has decreased, from 1.7 per cent annually over the past 30 years to a projected 1.1 per cent annually until 2030, we have reached a critical mass of 7.6 billion people alive on the planet today, so even a slower rate of increase amounts to a continuing huge explosion in human population.

Let's focus on Indonesia, as it is one of the countries worst hit. Indonesia encompasses 18,000 islands and its rainforest is the third largest on earth, after the Amazon and the Congo Basin. It is particularly important as it contains habitats where tigers, rhinos, orangutans and elephants still roam the same forests – a characteristic now sadly unique in the world. Pristine rainforests are being cut down to feed the country's poor, by allowing them to harvest the fertile ground left by the diverse ecosystem.

Indonesia has lost 80 per cent of its rainforest since the 1960s. In 2012 alone, Indonesia felled 8,400km² (3,243 miles²) of trees compared to the 4,600km² (1,776 miles²) lost in Brazil, even though the Amazon rainforest is four times larger. But how do you tell an impoverished Indonesian not to cut wood from the forest to warm his family, not to kill an orangutan for bushmeat that would feed his starving dependants for weeks, or not to catch a baby orangutan to sell to the exotic pet trade. Poverty and habitat loss go hand in hand. This country has seen the extinction of the Bali Tiger and the Javan Tiger, while the Sumatran Tiger, the last survivor of all the Indonesian tigers, has a population as low as 150 breeding pairs and declining.

Indonesia is the fourth largest country in the world in terms of population size, having 260 million inhabitants, with the majority of people living in poverty. They, quite understandably, could not care less, whether an animal is endangered or not – even though there might be scientists on the other side of the world who have lovingly dedicated their entire lives to research on the animal. They only care whether they have got enough to eat. They do not care whether they are destroying the habitat and ecosystem of multitudes of threatened mammals (135 out of a total of 515 species – Indonesia has more mammal species than any other country), they only care whether they have firewood for the night, for warmth and for cooking. And it is completely expected.

Even though there has been illegal logging in protected areas of the Indonesian rainforests, the government tends to turn a blind eye. That is because these rainforests are making the government rich. The majority of that wealth comes from the pulp and paper industry which answers an international demand for cheap paper, books, toilet paper, packaging and tissues. Pulp can also be manufactured into rayon, a fabric used to make clothes and sold all over the world. Other plantations are oil palm, which is used in hundreds of products, ranging from margarine and oven chips to cosmetics and even biodiesel. Plywood taken from the trees, whilst destroying the forest, also has a commercial value.

Due to scenarios such as these being replicated on a worldwide scale there are now 5,583 species listed as 'Critically Endangered' by the IUCN – the International Union for the Conservation of Nature – on its Red List. Species are listed according to their classification, and the range is as follows:

- Least Concern: lowest risk (44,148 species).
- Near Threatened: likely to become endangered in the near future (6,186).
- Vulnerable: high risk of endangerment in the wild (11,783).
- Endangered: high risk of extinction in the wild (8,455).
- Critically Endangered: extremely high risk of extinction in the wild (5,583).
- Extinct In The Wild: known only to survive in captivity, or as a established population outside its historic range (69).
- Extinct: no known individuals remaining (866).

Another measure that is used gauge the status of endangered species is CITES, which stands for the Convention on International Trade in Endangered Species of Wild Fauna and Flora, which came into being in 1975 and brings together the international community of most governments. The majority of species in this book are listed in Appendix I of CITES, which relates to species that are vulnerable to extinction. Commercial trade in these species, caught from the wild, is illegal. All the species in this book are Critically Endangered with the exception of the Blue Whale which is listed as Endangered.

TURNING THINGS AROUND?

On a positive note, there are millions of people at work around the world attempting to halt loss of biodiversity and the extinction of species. And while it may not always be possible to make a difference, in some cases the key to success has been to turn a conservation issue into a win-win situation for the threatened species in question and for the human population living in the vicinity.

For example, showing what can be achieved, ecotourism is now thriving in Uganda with more than 20,000 visits to see the Mountain Gorillas in 2008, bringing in US$8 million. It is thought that each gorilla will generate US$3.5 million in its lifetime. This is enough to fund the Virunga National Park and also cover a significant percentage of the entire country's conservation budget.

Other success stories from around the world include the following, which can all be read about in much greater detail in the chapters of this book:

The very positive action taken by the Fijian government, which has dedicated the entire island of Yadua Taba to the conservation of the Fiji Crested Iguana with fantastic results. They have removed non-native goats and stopped the practice of clearing the forest by fire. Both of these actions allow the forest to flourish, while the removal of invasive non-native *Leucaena* trees has now begun. There has been a 10-20 per cent increase in forest cover and the iguana is flourishing, with numbers up to 4,000. Plans have been put in place to create other protected island habitats.

Ecotourism in the little town of Mayumba in Gabon is helping the Leatherback Turtle population to thrive. The beaches around this town, which has been given national park status, provide nesting grounds to thousands of female turtles each year.

The Lemur Leaf Frog is being successfully bred in captivity, and thanks to increased water capacity through the provision of artificial ponds, it is now a common sight at the Guayaćan Nature Reserve in Costa Rica.

The California Condor was declared extinct in the wild in 1987, and the remnant population of 27 birds was taken into captivity. It is still one of the world's rarest birds, but as of December 2016 there were 446 condors alive, either in the wild or in captivity.

This is only the beginning; so much is being done in the way of conservation and there are many unsung heroes. People are dedicating their entire lives for the preservation of a particular species. But what's needed is to get local people to see that there is more money in preserving a habitat and saving an animal rather than killing it. Even though there may be less money for the individual, the collective will benefit and this is what will hold communities together. This is a tall order when poachers are even going into zoos, killing a rhino and taking its horn in order to make a fortune, but including communities in the conservation effort and making it financially profitable for them will radically change the situation. Time is running out for many of the species listed in this book. Rewarding communities will give real value to the conservation effort.

Siamese Crocodile.

Chinese Giant Salamander

Andrias davidianus

Key Facts

» World's biggest amphibian. Belongs to the family Cryptobranchidae, which diverged from other amphibians 170 million years ago.

» Now extremely rare in the wild due to unsustainable levels of hunting and collection by humans for food. Once much more widespread in China, today it occurs only in a small number of river basins.

» In captivity individuals have reached the age of 60 years. Millions are kept in farms in China but they are difficult to breed, meaning that stock must be replenished from wild-caught animals.

» Captive specimens that have been pumped full of hormones, and carry disease, are reintroduced back into the wild without any conservation expertise.

» Breeding is triggered when water temperatures rise to 20°C (68°F) and the salamanders cease feeding. This makes the species particularly prone to the effects of global warming.

THE BIGGEST AMPHIBIAN

The Chinese Giant Salamander is the largest amphibian in the world, reaching a maximum length of 180cm (5.9ft), although specimens that size are not often seen today. It is totally aquatic and lives in craggy mountain streams and lakes in China. Habitat loss, pollution and overcollection are its greatest threats as it is seen as a luxury food item in China and is also used for traditional medicine. There has been an 80 per cent drop in numbers since the 1950s.

170-MILLION-YEAR LINEAGE

The species is among three known extant giant salamanders belonging to the family Cryptobranchidae, the others being the Japanese Giant Salamander (*Andrias japonicus*) and the American Hellbender (*Cryptobranchus alleganiensis*). Predecessors of the Cryptobranchidae diverged from the lineage of other amphibians which are alive today about 170 million years ago during the Jurassic Period. Therefore giant salamanders are known as 'living fossils'.

CHARACTERISTICS

This huge amphibian is totally aquatic. It has a wide, compressed head with tiny, lidless eyes on the top, giving the animal inferior vision. It has pairs of tubercles dotted around the head. About 60 per cent of its wide, flat body is made up of its tail and the skin is rough with small bumps. The skin can excrete a gummy white substance that repulses predators. With the adults lacking gills, this skin also acts as a breathing device with oxygen being taken in and carbon dioxide released. The skin is generally dark brown with irregular spotted marks, although it can be dark red, green or even black. The two pairs legs are of similar length.

On average an adult salamander will weigh 25–30kg (55–66lb) and grow to a length of 115cm (3.77ft). The largest individual recorded was a farmed salamander in Zhangjiajie in 2007 which measured 180cm (5.9ft). Due to excessive poaching, salamanders in the wild are substantially smaller than this.

The salamander has been known to bark, hiss, whine or cry. The crying is particularly similar to that of a crying child, and the species' name in China reflects this, translating as 'infant fish'.

DIET AND CANNIBALISM

Crustaceans and fish make up the bulk of their diet. They have many tiny teeth, enabling them to firmly hold their prey, which they catch with a quick sideways crack of the mouth. They strongly depend on their sense of smell and touch as their vision is so poor. They also eat millipedes, insects, horsehair worms, frogs and toads and their tadpoles, and Asiatic water shrews. Cannibalism is a reasonably regular occurrence with a study of salamander diet in the Qinling-Dabashan range showing Chinese Giant Salamander remains in 5 out of 79 specimens, making up 28 per cent of the total food weight in the entire study.

SENSORY NODES AND FEEDING

Sensory nodes run though the body from head to tail, which enable the salamander to detect the slightest movement. The animals are active at night but become increasingly diurnal during the breeding season. During the day they rest in the rocky crevices. When the water reaches 20°C (68°F) they cease feeding.

TERRITORIES AND BREEDING

Chinese Giant Salamanders are territorial with a male having a larger territory of 40m² (430ft²) compared to 30m² (320ft²) for a female. Mating season is July to September when water temperatures rise to 20°C (68°F). Males compete savagely, often to the death. The female lays 400–500 eggs, connected like a beaded necklace, in an aquatic chamber and then quickly leaves. The male will fertilise the eggs and aggressively guard the chamber for 50–60 days until the eggs hatch. The eggs double in size from 7–8mm (0.28–0.31in) by taking in water. When the larvae are born they are 3cm

(1.2in) long and will have exterior gills until the age of three years. When they have grown to 40–50cm (16–20in), usually around the age of 5–6 years, they will be sexually mature. In captivity, individuals have reached the age of 60 years, but it is not known how long wild salamanders live for.

HISTORIC AND PRESENT RANGE

Once found throughout central, south-western and southern China, the Chinese Giant Salamander now occurs only in the river basins of the Yangtze, Yellow and Pearl Rivers. It lives in clear streams with boulders and rocky crevices beside the banks. Most live in forested regions at altitudes of 300–800m (1,000–2,600ft). They favour narrow, cool, fast-flowing streams about 6–7m (20–23ft) wide and 1m (3.3ft) deep, but also inhabit mountain lakes.

CAPTIVE BREEDING FOR FOOD

About 2.6 million Chinese Giant Salamanders were recorded as being kept in farms in the province of Shaanxi in 2007. Farming provides many Chinese families with an income, and these farms accounted for 70 per cent of Chinese output in 2012. However, they are finding it difficult to breed from second-generation captive-bred individuals, meaning that they must replenish their stock from more wild-caught salamanders. Release of captive-bred salamanders is endorsed by the government but there have been cases of diseases, such as Ranavirus, affecting the wild population.

OVERHUNTING AND CONSERVATION EFFORTS

Populations of the Chinese Giant Salamander have decreased rapidly since the 1950s due to overhunting and habitat destruction. From the 1980s efforts have been put in place to help conserve the species by setting up 14 nature reserves covering 355,000 hectares (877,225 acres).

Salamander meat is a luxury item, making it an attractive target for poachers, and despite the designation of reserves, poaching continues to be a massive problem. There is not enough legal protection around the species, with fines for poaching at about 50 Yuan (US$8). The black market will pay a hundred times more than that for a salamander which has been caught, making it a very strong incentive for the poachers. Restaurants charge US$250–400 per kg (US$115–180 per lb).

Poaching methods and reintroductions

Unfortunately giant salamanders are extremely easy to catch. Poachers use a bow hook assembled from bamboo, with a frog or small fish as a lure, and make sure the amphibian does not die. Another common practice is for the poacher to kill the salamander using pesticides and then sell the meat.

The capture of wild salamanders by farms is not regulated or managed, and due to the lack of breeding success in the second-generation of captive-bred animals, the wild population is being severely depleted. Captive specimens that have been pumped full of hormones are reintroduced back into the wild without any conservation expertise. Many salamanders also escape from farms back into the wild and carry disease which spreads through wild populations.

Industry and pollution

In recent decades large swathes of salamander habitat have been adversely affected by industrial processes. Dams cause rivers to dry up and siltation degrades ecosystems by dirtying the water. Deforestation in neighbouring areas creates soil erosion and run-off into the rivers, depleting the quality of the water. This compromises the salamander's ability to breath.

Mining and farming both affect water quality, introducing pesticides and other chemicals. Macronutrients in rivers create algal blooms which obscure the water and create a rise in temperature. They also reduce oxygen levels in the water, which can be fatal for the salamanders. As a result the species is now extremely rare.

The Chinese Giant Salamander is also prone to global warming since it does not feed in temperatures greater than 20°C (68°F).

Future prospects

A period of about 15 years between generations makes it very difficult for the species to recover from losses. In recent years there are not only less

populations recorded, with smaller numbers in those populations, but the size of the individuals has also decreased. An unsustainable level of hunting by humans for the luxury food market is the primary cause of this.

Lemur Leaf Frog

Hylomantis lemur

Key Facts

» Tiny frog, with adult male measuring 3cm (1.2in) in length and weighing only 2g (0.07oz).

» Has antimicrobial skin peptides and exhibits anti-cancer and anti-bacterial functions.

» Endemic to Colombia, Costa Rica and Panama, living in subtropical, tropical moist lowland or montane forest, in places with extremely high levels of precipitation.

» Steep decline in population due to a combination of habitat loss and the fatal chytrid fungus.

» Captive breeding has been successful and the scheme has extended to many countries.

» The wild population at Guayacán Rainforest Reserve, Costa Rica, has increased thanks to the introduction of artificial ponds for breeding.

REMAINING POPULATIONS

This tiny frog is endemic to Colombia, Costa Rica and Panama. One of the rarest frogs known to science, it lives in subtropical or tropical moist lowland forest and montane forest. These are extremely humid places, having a mean annual precipitation of 2.5–3.5m (8.2–11.5ft). Populations of the Lemur Leaf Frog in each country are very limited. Colombia has three populations, and only the one at Fila Asunción is said to be a large breeding colony. The population in Panama has declined to such an extent in the last few years that the species has been classified as Critically Endangered by the IUCN.

CHAMELEON CHARACTERISTICS

The Lemur Leaf Frog is tiny and can easily sit on the end of a human finger. During the daytime, when it will often rest on the underside of a leaf, it is bright green with brown speckles. Its hands, feet and sides are yellow, and its belly and throat white. It has huge eyes with a silvery-white iris, which is encircled by a black ring. The vertical pupils indicate nocturnal behaviour. The frogs are most active after dark, which is when their body will change from green to reddish-brown.

A WALKER, NOT A HOPPER

These frogs look very frail. They are unusual among leaf frogs in that they do not exhibit inter-digital webbing between the toes. The arms and legs are very thin, lacking muscle so that the amphibian tends to walk on all four limbs rather than pushing off from the hind-legs in a leaping movement. This walking movement lends it the name 'lemur', after the mammal lemur which also walks on all four limbs.

OTHER FEATURES

The species exhibits sexual dimorphism, with the female being larger than the male. In terms of length, males are 3–3.5cm (1.2–1.4in) and females

4–4.5cm (1.6–1.8in), while males weigh on average 2g (0.07oz) compared to 4g (0.14oz) for females.

Lemur Leaf Frog diet requires further research, although it is thought that they are chiefly insect eaters. Similar species typically consume insects, snails and other small invertebrates.

MATING BEHAVIOUR

Mating takes place throughout the lengthy rainy season, predominantly in spring or summer. The breeding season is 'prolonged', and mating takes place unceasingly throughout this period. The male finds the leaf surface of a plant or shrub next to or overhanging water. He will call to females, giving out a series of clicks to grab their attention. A female will respond by going over to the male and carrying him on her back to a spawning location. This is typically on the underside of a smooth leaf that hangs over water. A clutch of 15–30 eggs are set down. The Lemur Leaf Frog is unusual in that it does not roll the leaf-side around the clutch. Instead the eggs fall or are washed off into the water below.

EGGS AND TADPOLES

The blue-green eggs are laid on a leaf in a characteristic mass of jelly. They will fall into the water after approximately 7–10 days, but this depends on local conditions such as temperature, food and water supply. The metamorphosis from tadpole to frog takes a further 90–150 days. Tadpoles are bluish and their body is opaque with see-through dorsal and ventral fins.

THREATS – FUNGUS AND HABITAT LOSS

The decline in population of the Lemur Leaf Frog, which in Panama is estimated to be 80 per cent in the last 15 years, is considered to be primarily due to a combination of habitat loss and the fatal chytrid fungus.

The chytrid fungus is a global problem, killing many amphibian species and bringing many populations and even entire species to the point of extinction.

The Lemur Leaf Frog is affected, but because its skin does not dry out in sunlight it is able to bask in the midday sun, thereby creating enough heat to kill off the fungus.

CAPTIVE BREEDING SUCCESS

Captive breeding has been successful so far. Work done at the Manchester Museum in the UK has been so effective that it has enabled Lemur Leaf Frogs to be distributed to zoological centres across the world. Bristol Zoo Gardens in the UK has created a European studbook using DNA samples taken in 2015 and 2016 and manages captive breeding across Europe. Atlanta Botanical Garden in the USA has had extremely good results with captive breeding and has sent Lemur Leaf Frogs to 15 different countries.

One drawback of captive breeding is that the Lemur Leaf Frog can suffer lesions because of a vitamin A deficiency caused by a primarily insect diet.

MORE PONDS, MORE FROGS

The Costa Rican Amphibian Research Centre commenced Lemur Leaf Frog conservation work in 2003 with an in-situ project in the Guayácan Rainforest Reserve. This involved increasing the water capacity for breeding by introducing artificial ponds to protected sites. Plastic trays 1–2m (3.3–6.6ft) wide were placed at strategic points within the reserve, and 25–50 tadpoles were launched into each one as breeding founders. The following year, Lemur Leaf Frogs were found among the vegetation by these artificial ponds, mating and producing their own tadpoles.

In 2005, more artificial ponds were placed strategically in deeper areas of the forest and tadpoles were introduced to them. The Lemur Leaf Frog is now a common sight in the Guayácan Rainforest Reserve. Not only has the frog population become established at these sites, but is has now also spread and the species is found in neighbouring sections of the forest outside the reserve; sites where it has not been present since records began.

Mysteries still to be unravelled

The Lemur Leaf Frog has antimicrobial skin peptides and exhibits anti-cancer and anti-bacterial functions. There is still much research to be done in this area, but this little frog may have a number of hidden assets that could potentially be of use to humans.

Lemur Leaf Frog populations in Costa Rica and Panama appear to have different DNA, and perhaps represent different species.

Gharial

Gavialis gangeticus

KEY FACTS

» Wild population declined by 50 per cent between 1997–2006 with possibly only 235 individuals remaining, and occupying just 2 per cent of former range.

» Solitary hunter with no predators apart from humans.

» Wild Gharials live for 40–60 years and have a maximum recorded length of 7m (23ft).

» In 2004, 5,000 young Gharials were released back into the wild but the scheme ultimately failed due to severe habitat degradation.

» Today conservation efforts focus on the protection of Gharial habitat, which is increasingly lost to dams, barrages, irrigation canals and artificial embankments.

A CATASTROPHIC DECLINE

This fish-eating crocodile is found in the perennial rivers of Chambal, Girwa and Son in India, and in the Narayani River in Nepal. There are only thought to be 235 remaining in the wild, living in the calmer, deeper areas of fast-flowing rivers, occupying only 2 per cent of their former range. The species is threatened by loss of river habitat leading to habitat fragmentation, reduced fish populations and getting caught in fishing nets.

WHAT IS A GHARIAL?

Well known for its long, thin snout – a perfect adaptation for catching fish – the Gharial is one of three native crocodiles to be found in India, the others being the Mugger and Saltwater Crocodiles. The species is one of the largest crocodilians – a group consisting of alligators, crocodiles, caimans and others – with the largest recorded being a 7m (23ft) long individual that was hunted in 1924. It is thought that specimens of this size were more common in the past, but today we typically expect reptiles of 3.7–4.5m (12–15ft), weighing up to 1,000kg (2,200lb). Females tend to be slightly smaller than males. A wild Gharial will characteristically live for 40–60 years.

The crocodile is dark olive above, with darker speckling on the dorsal surfaces of the head, body and tail. The ventral surfaces are yellow or whitish. It is cold blooded and needs to warm up by basking in the sun on sand banks; returning to water to cool down.

Hatchlings reach the size of 1m (3.3ft) in 18 months. Their long, thin snout contains around 110 similar-looking, very pointed teeth with the largest being at the front. The muscular, laterally flattened tail gives them enormous power and agility in deep water, as does the webbing on the feet. However, unlike other crocodiles, on land they have trouble walking and can only push themselves forwards on their belly as their legs are not long enough to take their weight. For this reason they are one of the most aquatic of the crocodilians.

Males develop a hollow, bulbous nasal growth at the end of their snout when they become sexually mature at the age of ten. It is similar to an earthenware pot known as the ghara in Hindi, leading to the crocodile's common name.

A FISH-EATING SPECIALIST

Juvenile Gharials eat insects, frogs, tadpoles and small fish. Adults feed mainly on fish, especially larger predatory fish such as catfish. They use the 54–58 teeth in the upper jaw and 50–52 teeth in the lower jaw to grip prey and swallow it whole. There are sensory cells in the snout which detect vibrations from fish whilst the Gharial hides, waiting in large pools up to 4m (13ft) deep.

Gharials move to the surface to feed as a valve in the back of the throat prevents them from swallowing underwater. They herd the fish with their bodies, then catch their prey by whipping their head sideways and grabbing it in their mouth. They are solitary hunters with no predators apart from humans, who hunt them for their meat and hide. The Gharial can be aggressive to humans but is unable to inflict any harm due to the nature of its snout.

THE BUZZ OF COURTSHIP

The mating season extends from November to January. It starts with courtship rituals whereby males make hissing and buzzing sounds while they move around their territories. Many species of crocodile make a hissing noise, but the ghara on the end of the male Gharial's snout turns that into more of a buzz. The ghara also allows the sound to travel over great distances.

A male will accumulate a harem of females which he will defend from other males. Females show that they are willing to mate by raising their snout upwards. Mating takes place in the water.

A MONSOON HATCHING

The female uses her hind legs to dig a nest 50–60cm (20–24in) deep in a sand bank 1–5m (3.3–16.4ft) away from the waterline. A clutch of 50–95 eggs is laid, with these being the largest of any crocodilian species, each weighing 150g (5oz). She covers the nest with sand to protect from predators such as pigs, jackals, lizards, and mongooses.

The sex of the hatchlings, like that of other crocodiles, is related to temperature. The mother stays near the nest to guard it until hatching 71–93 days later. The young hatch in March or April, just before the rainy season. Upon hearing chirping calls from the nest, the female will start digging in order to release the hatchlings. Unlike other crocodiles, the female cannot carry the young to the water in her mouth, but she looks after them for several weeks until they learn the ways of the river. There is a risk of the young being washed down the river by the imminent rains.

POPULATION DECLINE DUE TO HABITAT LOSS

Gharial populations have decreased from an estimated 5,000–10,000 in 1946, to 235 in 2006, which is a 96–98 per cent decline in three generations. The population decline between 1997 and 2006 was 50 per cent, which led to the species being placed on the IUCN Red List.

Historically, Gharials were hunted for their skin, but this practice has largely ceased. Today it is the river habitat that is undergoing so many changes, which provides a constant challenge for Gharial survival. Their habitat is being lost as dams, barrages, irrigation canals and artificial embankments are being built. River courses are changing due to siltation and sand-mining. All these activities affect the flow of the river. Some areas dry out and as Gharials are so reliant upon water it makes life very difficult for them.

OTHER CAUSES OF POPULATION DECLINE

Changes in human fishing habits are also contributing to the Gharial's population decline. Traditionally throw nets, hook and line and scoop nets were used for fishing, but habits have changed and now the gill net is much more common. These nets are made from nylon and Gharials are commonly killed by becoming trapped in them. Although the Gharial is a sacred animal in India, many humans view them as competitors for fish stocks and have no qualms in killing them. Their eggs are collected for use in traditional medicine and adult males are hunted for the supposed aphrodisiacal properties of their snout.

HISTORICAL CONSERVATION – REWILDING GHARIALS

Project Crocodile was started in 1975 with the backing of the Indian government. Its aim was to focus on captive breeding and rearing so that young Gharials could be released into their natural habitat. The scheme saw 16 rehabilitation centres and five crocodile sanctuaries established between 1975 and 1982. By 2004, 12,000 Gharial eggs had been obtained from the wild, and through captive breeding, 5,000 Gharials of more than 1m (3.3ft) in length were released back into the wild. This project ultimately failed because habitat degradation had become so much of a problem in many areas that rewilding Gharials was not an option.

MODERN CONSERVATION – RECLAIMING HABITATS

Nowadays conservation efforts are focusing on the protection of Gharial habitats and the enforcement of the species' protected status. The education and involvement of local people in the conservation process is also key, and farmers, fishermen and many other people all share the need for a healthy river in order to thrive.

The good news is that captive Gharials were observed using artificial sand banks for nesting and basking. Some habitat managers have enjoyed a degree of success in using artificial sand banks in the wild, with Gharials using these in the same way that they would natural features. This gives some hope for the future in terms of the reclamation and reconstruction of degraded habitats.

MORE THAN ONE ENDANGERED SPECIES

Other important species that depend on the Gharial's riverine habitat include the Ganges River Dolphin, a dozen species of turtle, Smooth-coated Otter, large numbers of different river birds, Mugger Crocodiles and fish such as the Mahseer and giant catfish. All are at risk.

PREHISTORIC ROOTS

The lineage of the Gharial goes back to the time of the dinosaurs, with the earliest Gharial dying out at the end of the Cretaceous Period, and others surviving to the early Eocene. The modern Gharial evolved at around this time, living in the estuaries of Africa. The Gharial today is the last in this prehistoric line and the only surviving species in the family Gavialidae.

Siamese Crocodile

Crocodylus siamensis

KEY FACTS

» Extinct in 99 per cent of range, which formerly spanned much of South-East Asia.

» Small and apparently declining population of 200–400 individuals in Cambodia is all that remains.

» Male can reach a length of 4m (13ft) and weigh 350kg (770lb).

» Commercial farms in South-East Asia hold more than 700,000 Siamese Crocodiles, although the majority of these are hybrids with the Saltwater Crocodile.

» An unhybridized Siamese Crocodile is not considered a danger to humans.

REMNANT POPULATIONS

A small to medium-sized freshwater crocodile which thrives in slow-moving, sheltered parts of rivers, lakes, streams, rainforest lagoons, seasonal oxbow lakes, swamplands and marshes. During May to September when the heavy monsoon rains come in, the crocodile will explore a wider territory of large lakes and waterways, moving back to its usual habitat once water-levels have receded.

Historically the range of the Siamese Crocodile encompassed Indonesia (Borneo and possibly Java), Thailand, Myanmar, Brunei, East Malaysia, Laos and Vietnam. Now it is thought to be just Cambodia that holds small, isolated populations in Vireak Chey National Park in the north-east of the country and remote parts of the Cardamom Mountains in the west. Small populations may exist elsewhere.

SHAPE AND SIZE

This crocodile has a relatively wide snout which implies a generalist feeding strategy. This snout is comparatively flat and of medium length. There is a raised, bony crest on top of the cranial plate between the eyes. The iris is green. Its body is olive-green, dappled black with some divergence to dark green. The underside is consistently white and free from any black patches. The young will exhibit dark crossbands on the tail and trunk, resembling the paler Saltwater Crocodile, which has a golden-tan body with similar black stripes on the body and tail. The juvenile Siamese Crocodile will lose these stripes as they grow.

Typically Siamese Crocodiles grow to a maximum of 3m (10ft), although unusually large individuals can occur in any species of crocodilian and big males can reach a length of 4m (13ft), weighing 350kg (770lb). Captive individuals are usually longer than those in the wild, although many are hybridised with the larger Saltwater Crocodile.

PRACTICALLY EXTINCT IN THE WILD

The Siamese Crocodile is now absent from 99 per cent of its former range. Prior to 1992 very little research had been carried out into its distribution, reproductive biology and numbers. It was declared practically extinct in the wild in 1992. In that year surveys found 30 sites in Cambodia where the species was living in the wild, with an estimated population of 200–400 crocodiles in total, although it was thought that numbers were falling. A very small population was found in Thailand but this was considered not to be viable for breeding, so theoretically the population there will become extinct.

No recent surveys have been conducted in Malaysia, Brunei or Myanmar. Very few populations still exist and since 1992 valuable research has been undertaken, although population estimates are still difficult to ascertain. All in all the situation is pretty bleak.

COMMERCIAL FARMING

There are more than 700,000 animals carrying Siamese Crocodile genes living on commercial crocodile farms in South-East Asia, although the majority of these are hybrids with other species such as Saltwater Crocodile.

Commercial farming has caused a reduction in the wild population of Siamese Crocodiles. It has had a hugely beneficial impact on the economy of certain parts of Cambodia, for example in 1998 Tonlé Sap Lake had 396 farms holding over 20,000 crocodiles. The crocodiles have been exported to many countries including Thailand, Vietnam and China.

RELATIONSHIP WITH HUMANS

A pure, unhybridized Siamese Crocodile is not considered a danger to humans and there are no known records of an unprovoked attack. Where restocking takes place the hope is that people and crocodiles can live together without incident. Local people regard the crocodile as sacred and aim to protect it. The Siamese Crocodile enjoys a wealthy cultural heritage in Cambodia going back to ancient Angkorian times and stone carvings of crocodiles can still be seen in the temples today. Providing habitat is maintained and protected, there is a good chance of success with rewilding.

BREEDING

In captivity a female is ready to breed at 10 years of age. She will build a nest from plant debris and combine it with mud to form a mound. Breeding takes place during the wet season, usually in May to June. Between 15–60 eggs are laid and the female will watch over them for approximately 80 days. When they start to hatch she will help the young to break free from the eggs and will carry them to water in her mouth.

DIET

The broad snout suggests a generalist feeding approach, although little is known about the feeding habits of wild populations. In captivity an adult's diet consists mainly of fish and snakes, but they are also known to take reptiles, amphibians, insects, birds and small mammals.

THREATS

Wild populations are under threat from habitat loss and degradation. This is mainly due to the conversion of wetland and rainforest habitat for agriculture, the use of chemical fertilisers and pesticides in rice production, and growth in the number of cattle. Land mines and the aerial bombardment utilised during the Vietnam War has had lasting consequences in Vietnam, Cambodia and Laos. River systems have been irreparably altered because of hydroelectric dams, with 50 per cent greater flow in the dry season than normal. It is thought that half the remaining breeding population of wild Siamese Crocodiles will become extinct in the next ten years.

On farms the Siamese Crocodile is hybridised with the Saltwater Crocodile, which is the largest of all living reptiles. This produces offspring with a better quality of skin and higher growth rates, which equates to an increased yield.

PROTECTION

Historically, the Siamese Crocodile was aggressively hunted for its skin and to sell to commercial farms. In 1945 the French colonial administration in Cambodia abolished hunting of the species, only for the the Khmer Rouge (1975–79) to remove this protection. However, the Fishery Law of 1987 forbade the catching, selling and transportation of crocodiles. Even so, the greatest threat the Siamese Crocodile faces is still hunting for its skin.

BREEDING IN CAPTIVITY

In 1999 the Cambodian Crocodile Conservation Program (CCCP) worked alongside the Phnom Tamao Wildlife Rescue Centre based in Phnom Penh, Cambodia. They conducted DNA analysis of the 69 crocodiles in the centre and discovered 35 to be pure-bred Siamese Crocodiles. They went on to organise a captive-breeding scheme. This has been successful and since 2012 more than 50 Siamese Crocodiles have been freed into community protected habitats to join and strengthen the existing wild population.

In 2011 the Wildlife Conservation Society (WCS) in Laos hatched 20 Siamese Crocodiles. The organisation is working with local residents to preserve, maintain and safeguard the biodiversity of the whole landscape, with the crocodiles and many other species set to benefit.

REINTRODUCTION TO THE WILD

Wild Siamese Crocodiles have all but disappeared from Thailand, but there is hope that a population can be reinstated. Reintroduction depends on maintaining protected habitat and working with crocodile farms to ensure genetic purity. Thailand has the most developed habitat management system and the greatest availability of farm-raised crocodiles. Work is also being conducted in Vietnam to reinstate the crocodile in a similar manner.

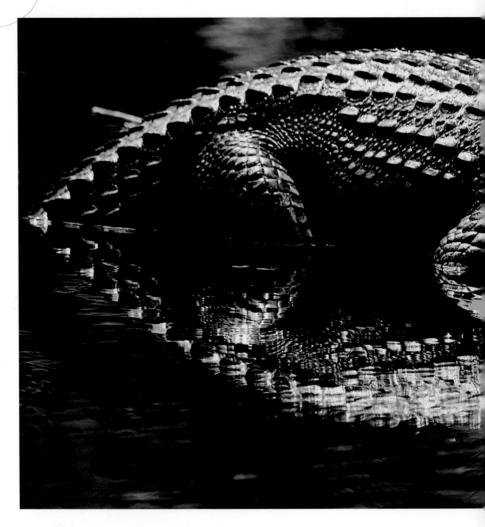

FURTHER RESEARCH

Research is required regarding the taxonomy of all freshwater crocodiles in South-East Asia and the Indo-Malaysian Archipelago. At present the situation is unclear and results yielded would greatly aid conservation

work. Although the prospects for the Siamese Crocodile are far from certain, work done in the last ten years has created optimism for the future of the species.

Orinoco Alligator

Crocodylus intermedius

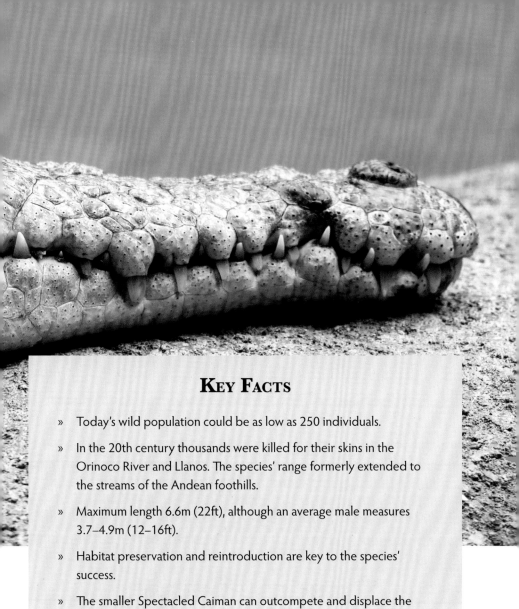

KEY FACTS

» Today's wild population could be as low as 250 individuals.

» In the 20th century thousands were killed for their skins in the Orinoco River and Llanos. The species' range formerly extended to the streams of the Andean foothills.

» Maximum length 6.6m (22ft), although an average male measures 3.7–4.9m (12–16ft).

» Habitat preservation and reintroduction are key to the species' success.

» The smaller Spectacled Caiman can outcompete and displace the Orinoco Alligator.

LARGEST PREDATOR IN THE AMERICAS

The final remnant population of the Orinoco Alligator is very small and can be found in Colombia and Venezuela. The species is classified as Critically Endangered due to the small size and restricted dispersal of the wild population, as well as the prevailing dangers from habitat destruction and hunting.

In the 19th and 20th centuries it suffered massive losses to its population due to extensive hunting for skins. It is the largest predator in the Americas and one of the largest living reptiles in the world. The Orinoco Alligator takes third place behind the Saltwater Crocodile, which has a length of 4.3-5.5m (14-18ft), and the Nile Crocodile which is broadly similar in length to the Orinoco Alligator but has a slightly greater mean mass. The Orinoco Alligator is the most highly endangered of all crocodilian species.

PRESENT RANGE

Once the Orinoco Alligator ranged from tropical evergreen forests to the streams of the Andean foothills. Now the sole riparian habitat that it occupies is the Llanos savannah and the seasonal freshwater tributaries of the Orinoco river. This freshwater riverine habitat is found in the middle and lower parts of the Orinoco river and seasonal short-term rivers are created when the savannah becomes waterlogged in the rainy season. These rivers disappear in the dry season; the water level drops and available habitat disappears. During this period the Orinoco Alligator will usually burrow into the mud where small amounts of water remain, although it can also move overland to search for areas of deeper water.

UNUSUAL SIGHTINGS

The Orinoco Alligator has been reported on the island of Trinidad, 240km (150 miles) north of Venezuela. Such records could possibly have occurred when individuals got swept out to sea during flooding, perhaps on buoyant mats of vegetation. It would also suggest that the Orinoco Alligator can tolerate the salinity of sea water.

GREEK ROOTS

The family name *Crocodylus* comes from the Greek 'krokodeilos' which means 'pebble worm', referring to the outward appearance of the alligator. The specific name *intermedius* is derived from the Latin and alludes to the shape of the alligator's snout, which is 'intermediate' between the rounded snout common to most alligators. and the parallel-sided snout belonging to the Gharial. Crocodiles, in contrast to alligators, typically exhibit V-shaped, or triangular-shaped snouts.

HISTORIC AND PRESENT LENGTH

In the past Orinoco Alligators were larger in size due to greater food availability and resources. One shot in 1800 measured 6.6m (22ft) in length. Large-scale hunting for skins removed the largest specimens, leaving the smaller Orinoco Alligators that are alive at present.

The largest Orinoco Alligator known today measures 5.2m (17ft) in length, but males average 3.5–4.7m (12–16ft), weighing 385–635kg (840–1,400lb). While sexual dimorphism is not so great as in other crocodilians, the female is still smaller on average at 3.0–3.2m (9.8–10.8ft) and weighing 225–316kg (496–698lb).

CHARACTERISTICS

The snout is proportionately long and narrow, with 68 teeth. It is thinner than the comparable American Crocodile. Captive held individuals show a snout that curves marginally upwards. They have short, powerful legs, with a long, muscular tail. There are three variations: 'mariposo', which is greenish on the body and has black dorsal markings; 'amarillo', which is the most usual, with a pale tan body and dispersed dark patches; and 'negro', which is consistently dark. The alligator can change shade over long periods of time. This has been observed in captivity and is also seen in other species that can alter the amount of melanin in their skin.

DIET

Due to the small population it has been difficult to survey the reptile's biology in any great depth. Some suggest it has a diet consisting mainly of fish. However, it is the apex predator in its range, hunting both aquatic and terrestrial species, and any species is potential prey. In the water, it kills large predatory fish, aided by its proportionately narrow snout. Even though it has an elongated skull, the base of the snout is broad, indicating a more extensive diet. Terrestrial prey includes reptiles, birds, mammals, invertebrates, capybara and even domestic animals. Like other large crocodilians, it will eat smaller crocodiles, which includes caimans and young of its own species. The young have a diet of small fish and invertebrates.

While attacks on humans have been documented, the Orinoco Alligator is less aggressive than other crocodile species of a similar size. The species lives in small populations away from human settlements, so it is unlikely to cause any harm.

REPRODUCTION

During the annual dry season the river is lower, exposing sandbanks in which the alligators dig holes to lay their eggs. The alligator pair mates in the dry season, with the nesting holes being excavated in January to February each year. The female lays 15–70 eggs, with the average number being 40. These are sometimes taken by predators such as tegu lizards and vultures.

The gestation period lasts for 14 weeks. As the water-levels begin to rise and the wet season begins, the young hatch during the night and call to their mother. She scoops them out of the sand and transfers them to the water in her mouth. The young alligators are preyed upon by vultures, tegu lizards, caimans, jaguars, coatis, anacondas and other carnivores. The mother will defend her young for at least one year, and sometimes for up to three years. Females become more aggressive during the nesting season and what is normally a relaxed alligator should not be approached during this time.

HUMAN THREATS

Humans are the main threat to the Orinoco Alligator. Thousands of these animals in the Orinoco River and Llanos wetlands were massacred for their hide, in particular during the period from the 1940s to the 1960s. Hunters visited in the dry season, snatching the alligators from their burrows.

As a result of overhunting the species was teetering on the edge of extinction. In the 1970s it was granted protected status, but numbers are still dangerously low. It is safeguarded by CITES Appendix I but still faces serious threats today. These include the capture of juveniles for sale in the wild animal trade, the pollution of their riverine habitat, and the proposal for a dam in the upper Orinoco River area. In addition Orinoco Alligators are illegally killed so that their meat can be sold for food or their teeth used for supposed health reasons, while their eggs are also collected for food. Although the species is protected, it is not always effectively enforced.

THREATS FROM OTHER SPECIES

Other species are posing a risk too; there is a surge in the population of the smaller Spectacled Caiman which can displace the Orinoco Alligator from its food source, as it has a greater population and faster breeding rates. More survey work on the natural history and ecological relationships within the Orinoco river basin would substantially help conservation work.

Population today

It is not known how many Orinoco Alligators remain in the wild. Estimates range from 250–1,500 animals. The greatest population, living in Cojedes and Sarare in Venezuela, has less than 500 individuals, while a small number of minor subpopulations exist. It is suspected that increased survey work would reveal hidden populations in locations that are not in close proximity to human settlements.

Conservation

Habitat preservation work is taking place in Venezuela with reintroduction plans. It is important to provide effective protection for the existing wild population. A reintroduction initiative is also being working on in Colombia. The Orinoco Alligator has a comparable skin to that of the American Crocodile which, although protected under federal law in the US, is not on CITES Appendix I – the American Crocodile is on Appendix II, whereby trade is controlled rather than illegal.

Orinoco Alligators in captivity

Figures from 2007 stated that 50 Orinoco Alligators were held in zoos, including 35 at Dallas World Aquarium in the USA. Venezuela also holds a significant number in captive breeding sites. Six of these sites operate in Venezuela today, but they are burdened with low funds and staff shortages. In the early 1990s a notable number of hatchlings were freed into Venezuelan national parks and into private ranchlands in the Llanos regions where ecotourism is key to the local economy.

Fiji Crested Iguana

Brachylophus vitiensis

Key Facts

» Endemic to dry forests on a few islets in western Fiji.

» Population has diminished by 80 per cent in the past 40 years.

» Hunting by humans for food has largely ceased.

» Largest remnant population of more than 4,000 iguanas is on the island of Yadua Taba. Introduced goats and *Leucaena* trees that endanger the forest habitat are being removed.

» As a result of a failed poaching attempt in 2002, human access to Yadua Taba is restricted to researchers.

» Deviulau Island, which has many suitable food trees for the iguana, is unable to sustain a high population due to the presence of feral cats.

Protected status on Yadua Taba

The Fiji Crested Iguana is endemic to a few of the islands of western Fiji in the South Pacific. The species inhabits dry rain-shadow habitats including tropical beach forests and dry forests that only occur on certain islands. These forests are particularly threatened habitats in the Pacific.

The largest population, numbering 4,000 iguanas, lives on the larger island of Yadua Taba, which was designated as a national sanctuary in 2002 and is a place where the reptiles are afforded legal protection. Feral goats have been removed and the practice of clearing the forest by using fire has been stopped in order to preserve habitat. An additional rule states that no iguana that has left the island is allowed to return, to prevent spread of disease and parasites.

Also in 2002 five Fiji Crested Iguanas were stolen from Yadua Taba. Luckily the poacher was caught at the airport by customs officers before boarding an international flight. As a result of this crime, human access to the island is now limited to researchers only, with no other visitors allowed, including tourists.

Other island refuges

About 80 Fiji Crested Iguanas live on the small island of Macuata, while elsewhere in Fiji they can be found on Deviulau, Mouriki, Waya, Qalito and Malolo Levu. In the past the species could be found at altitudes up to 500m (1,640ft) above sea-level, but today most populations are restricted to altitudes up to 100m (330ft) above sea-level.

A recent discovery

The Fiji Crested Iguana was first documented in 1979 by Dr John Gibbons, who discovered the species while conducting research on the superficially similar Fiji Banded Iguana (*Brachylophus fasciatus*) that is also native to Fiji. He noticed several differences between the two species. The Fiji Crested Iguana has three thin white bands that pass over its back, while the Fiji Banded Iguana has wider blue bands. The Fiji Crested Iguana is bigger, weighing up to 300g (0.66lb) and reaching a length of 75cm (30in). It also has a spiny crest running down its back, with the spines measuring up to 1.5cm (0.58in). The Fiji Crested Iguana is also known to change from green to blackish very quickly when excited.

WARNINGS TO PREDATORS

The Fiji Crested Iguana is at home in the trees of the dry forest, moving easily between overlapping branches by using its long toes and tail to maintain equilibrium. Its skin will change to a different shade when threatened, although the degree of change will depend upon the severity of the danger. Bright green is the norm for a relaxed iguana, dark green would suggest a hazardous situation, and black indicates an acute threat. The iguana has further tricks up it sleeve if a predator is not already scared – it will inflate its neck, nod its head and ultimately leap towards the predator or threat.

DELICIOUS TROPICAL DIET

The tropical dry forests of western Fiji offer a varied menu and research shows that the same plants are eaten throughout the year with few seasonal shifts. The iguanas feed on the leaves, shoots, and flowers of trees and shrubs, with a particularly strong appetite for the flowers of the Vau tree (*Hibiscus tiliaceus*).

Diet varies between populations on different islands. For example, the Cevua tree (*Vavaea amicorum*) is considered to be the most important food source, making up 40 per cent of the dry forest in Yadua Taba, although this species is absent from Monuriki. A further study found that 63 per cent of trees on Yadua Taba provided food sources for the iguana, whilst this amounted to only 2 per cent on Monuriki. Forests on Monuriki are currently recovering from 30 years of exhaustive goat grazing and systematic burning during the dry season.

BREEDING AND LONG INCUBATION

Iguanas are egg-layers. For the Fiji Crested Iguana mating takes place in January, with 4–6 large white leathery eggs being laid in March or April. The female guards the eggs until they hatch 8–9 months later, at the beginning of the wet season in October to November. This is among the lengthiest incubation periods known in reptiles. A brown dot appears on the surface of the egg, which indicates where the iguana's head will emerge. The hatchlings gain fluids by licking moist foliage.

EXTINCTION LOOMS

Although populations currently exist on a total of eight islands, the Fiji Crested Iguana is facing extinction on all but Yadua Taba and perhaps Macuata. Populations of the reptile are thought to have diminished by 80 per cent in 40 years – the equivalent to 2–3 iguana generations – and they have disappeared from various islands where they were known to have lived in the 1980s.

MAINTAINING HABITAT

The species faces primary threats of habitat loss by the burning of the dry forest it lives in, storms, agricultural conversion to plantations and pasture, and conflict with feral goats. Goats were bought to Fiji in 1972 to help local people, and their population increased to more than 200 by the late 1970s. They feed on trees and shrubs, in the process destroying the iguanas' habitat.

When the Fiji Crested Iguana was first discovered, decisions were made to stop the burning of the forest and to remove the goats. Non-native and invasive *Leucaena* trees have endangered the future of the forest, but the Fiji government has put in place schemes to eliminate them. The forest area has enlarged by 10–20 per cent and is now a leading example of Pacific dry forest.

RATS, CATS AND OTHER THREATS

Hunting of Fiji Crested Iguanas by humans for food has died out, but other threats include predation by virulent non-native Black Rats (*Rattus rattus*), mongooses and feral cats. These animals also eat iguana eggs and need to be removed from the reptile's habitat as the goats were. Deviulau Island, which is made up of 23 hectares (57 acres), has a good number of food trees for the iguana but it is unable to sustain a high population due to the presence of feral cats.

The expansion of villages due to a rising human population and the building of facilities for tourists also pose dangers to the iguanas through exacerbating the degradation and loss of habitat. Due to all these concerns, there are not many places remaining in Fiji that maintain sufficient areas of undamaged dry forest.

Conservation success stories

The National Trust of Fiji has worked hard to protect the species – Yadua Taba has been a great success and has a thriving area of habitat for the Fiji Crested Iguana. However, the key islands of Yadua Taba and Monuriki, together with the less significant Deviulau, hold only 160 ha (395 acres) of Fiji

Crested Iguana habitat in total. Goats and Pacific Rats are being eradicated from Monuriki and captive-breeding and release projects on that island are being instigated. Although the iguana's situation is still looking precarious there are rays of hope for the future.

Geometric Tortoise

Psammobates geometricus

Key Facts

» Found only in very restricted range close to Cape Town, South Africa.

» Has very specialised diet and only able to live with a certain humidity, climate and soil type.

» 97 per cent of original habitat has been developed for urban and agricultural expansion, leaving just 4,000–5,000ha (9,885–12,355 acres).

» Only 2,000–3,000 of these tortoises remain – 75 per cent are in secured territory.

» Populations susceptible to fire, for example 250 Geometric Tortoises were killed by a single fire in 2012.

» Captive breeding has not been successful, so the main thrust of conservation work is to protect the tortoise's habitat

Rarest of the dozen

South Africa is home to 12 species of tortoise, which is the greatest number to be found in any country in the world. The Geometric Tortoise is found in a very tiny area just inland from Cape Town. It is the rarest species of the three in the genus *Psammobates* – the name means 'sand-loving'. The other two are the Tent Tortoise and the Serrated Tortoise, which look very similar to the Geometric Tortoise and are also indigenous to southern Africa, albeit with larger ranges and less specific habitat requirements.

A unique pattern

A strong, convex-shaped carapace (upper shell) helps to protect the Geometric Tortoise from predators. The shell is black overall, while each scute has a bright yellow centre with the yellow stripes radiating out from the middle like a star. This pattern is repeated on the underside of the tortoise, although it is slightly duller. The cryptic markings help the tortoise to blend in with its surroundings. Males grow to 10cm (4in) on average and females are slightly bigger, typically 12.5cm (5in) with a smaller tail and the carapace marginally upturned at the rear. The front feet have five toes while the hind feet have four.

Specialist habitat

The Geometric Tortoise inhabits winter rainfall areas which experience 30–60cm (12–24in) of annual precipitation. It is therefore found solely in the low-lying regions of the Upper Breede River Valley, Swartland and Ceres Valley in the Western Cape.

This habitat is known as the renosterveld, which is part of the fynbos biome and distinguished by a Mediterranean climate. The resnosterveld is made up of strandveld, intercoastal renosterveld and coastal renosterveld. The tortoises favour low-lying and well-drained regions with good shrub cover at about 50cm (20in) above ground.

The soils in these locations are typically acidic and poor in nutrients, giving rise to heathlands and shrublands. The tortoise has distinct dietary preferences and the wet habitat and topography of the area, which supports plant species such as restios, geophytes and grasses, is perfect for its needs.

A SHRINKING RANGE

This specialised habitat is being destroyed by urban expansion and agricultural development, particularly for vineyards and growing wheat. Only 3 per cent of the Geometric Tortoise's original habitat remains, which in real terms constitutes just 4,000–5,000 ha (9,885–12,355 acres), and there is a continuing threat to the remaining area. The population of Geometric Tortoises currently stands at 2,000 to 3,000 individuals, which require tracts of habitat that support them in terms of food, cover and nesting.

A population in the small Harmony Flats Reserve in Cape Town became extinct in the 1960s. Today there are populations in the Ceres Valley and the Tulbagh-Worcester Valley, and also in the coastal lowlands further south.

SPECIALISED DIET

The Geometric Tortoise eats flowers, shoots, leaves and other plant matter from a broad selection of native fynbos and renosterveld vegetation. Grasses such as *Themeda triandra*, *Briza maxima* and *Cynodon dactylon* are favoured, while its diet also features plant species such as *Crassula ciliate*, *Oxalis* species and indigenous geophyte species. In summer they specialise in perennial grasses, shrub and succulents, as the leafy green foods are not available until after rainfall. The tortoises are so specialised to feed on these plant types that they will die very quickly if their diet is altered, and as a result tortoises that are poached do not survive for long.

Other factors essential for their survival include the specific humidity, climate and soil type found in their range, meaning that the Geometric Tortoise is able to survive in only a very small area in this part of South Africa.

A RAINY HATCHING

The female Geometric Tortoise digs a hole every year and lays 1–2 clutches of 1–5 eggs, which it hides under vegetation. The eggs incubate for 5–8 months and hatch at the beginning of the winter rains. At this time the earth is less hard and there is an array of fresh new annual plants which offer food and shelter for the young. The tortoises are at a reduced risk from the natural fires that occur in the region during the dry period.

The young tortoises have a choice of small succulents, herbs and annual grasses, and will use the vegetation to protect them from the heat of the day or the chill of night. They are timid and hide in their shells or race for cover when they come across humans. Sexual maturity is reached at 8–10 years, which means that it takes a long time for a population to recover if it has been devastated by a fire.

THREATS

Main threats to the Geometric Tortoise come in the form of habitat degradation and fragmentation due to perennial fires. The renosterveld shrubland and fynbos biome are well suited to fire, however blazes have become ever more common as a result of drought, which could be an outcome of climate change. Extensive fires can cause the elimination of the Geometric Tortoise from an area, for example in 2012 blazes at a nature reserve killed 250 Geometric Tortoises – 50 per cent of the population at the site.

Predation by feral pigs, baboons, ostriches, Honey Badgers, White-necked Ravens and Pied Crows is a persistent problem. Pigs are thought to have adapted their behaviour, because although they never used to prey on the tortoise, they have recently learnt how to bite the shells in half.

Invasive non-native plant species are are pushing the native species out, creating a habitat that is not sustainable for the tortoise.

POACHERS FROM NEAR AND FAR

Local people eat the eggs of the tortoise and make decorative items to sell using the shells of the adults. Laws are in place to prevent the trapping of the tortoise and the collection of its eggs.

In 2002 a Czech poacher was captured just as he was about to board an international flight with a bag containing 23 Geometric Tortoises that were bound for the illegal pet trade. In addition the species has been advertised for sale on the Internet through a seller based in Germany. The tortoise is listed under Appendix I of CITES, banning international trade. The exotic pet trade is much less of a problem than it used to be for this species.

SAFEGUARDING THE TORTOISE

During captive breeding it has been found that the egg-laying cycle has diminished from two clutches per year to only one. This is attributed to climate change and to changes in the tortoise's already fragile habitat. Captive breeding has not proved to be successful, so the main thrust of conservation work is to protect the tortoise's habitat.

The Geometric Tortoise is safeguarded under Western Cape Provincial legislation, which is strongly disciplined and administered. At present 75 per cent of the population of this tortoise is in secured territory. The rest of the population is in the hands of private landowners, although plans are in place to acquire these areas for conservation use.

Angonoka Tortoise

Astrochelys yniphora

Key Facts

» Endemic to Madagascar, where only about 600 remain in the wild.

» Predicted to be extinct in the wild in 10–15 years.

» A female tortoise takes 20 years to reach sexual maturity.

» Fetches high prices in the pet trade, and poaching can cause serious damage to an already extremely fragile population.

» In 1996, 76 tortoises were stolen from a captive breeding centre.

» In 2014, one tenth of the world population of Angonoka Tortoises was seized from a smuggler at an international airport.

WHERE TO FIND ONE

This tortoise is endemic to Madagascar, where only about 600 remain in the wild, with numbers still declining. The population is centred around the Baly Bay area, near the town of Soalala in north-western Madagascar, in an area encompassing the Baie de Baly National Park. Just five very small and isolated populations remain, in terrain that is less than 50m (160ft) above sea-level.

AKA THE PLOUGHSHARE TORTOISE

The name Angonoka comes from a local word for the tortoise, but the species is also known as the Ploughshare Tortoise. This is due to the shape of the plates (scutes) on the bottom of the shell which protrude outwards and upwards between the front legs, curving up in the direction of the neck. This shape looks like the Madagascan ploughshare.

UNIQUE SHELLS

The carapace (upper shell) is very striking in appearance with unique patterning for each tortoise, in the same way as a human fingerprint. This has its downside as it makes the species popular in the international exotic pet trade. Prominent pale brown grooved rings of keratin grow on each scute or shell segment, while the space between the scutes is a darker brown.

The carapace of the male can measure up to 43cm (17in), but the average length when fully grown is 41cm (16in), while the average weight of a male is 10.3kg (23lb). Females are smaller, with an average carapace length of 37cm (14in) and weight of 8.8.kg (19lb). The difference in size makes distinguishing the sexes relatively straightforward.

BAMBOO AND BUSHPIG POO!

The tortoise's habitat around Baly Bay consists of dry deciduous forest, mangrove swamp and savannah with a large variation in terrain and plant life. The range includes bamboo scrub which is made up of various shrubs, savanna grasses, bamboo thickets and expansive rocky areas with little plant life. The tortoise seems to favour the bamboo scrub, and it loves to feed on dead bamboo leaves, although it has never been seen eating live bamboo. Elsewhere it will eat grasses in the rocky areas as well as shrubs and herbs in the thickets, and even feast on the droppings of bushpigs and carnivores. Their principal predator is the introduced bushpig, which feeds on tortoise eggs and young.

A LENGTHY REPRODUCTIVE CYCLE

Female Angonoka Tortoises do not reproduce until they reach 15–20 years old, which is a regrettable characteristic for a Critically Endangered species.

The breeding season – mating, egg-laying and hatching – takes place from 15 January to 30 May each year, making the most of the seasonal rainy season in Madagascar's tropical climate. Males are quite aggressive during breeding season when they compete for females. They ram, push and try to overturn each other using their ploughshare scales.

A female will lay 1–6 eggs per clutch and may lay four clutches each season. She will dig a pit with her back legs and lay her eggs, covering them with soil and then abandoning them. The young are self-sufficient immediately upon hatching, but as they are only as big as a pingpong ball they are vulnerable to attack from bushpigs.

Relatively low rates of fertility and success in hatching mean that for every breeding female an average of only four baby tortoises survive each year.

THREATS AND CONSERVATION

The predominant threats to the Angonoka Tortoise are the poaching of these beautiful creatures for the international pet trade and the clearing of land by fires for cattle grazing. The species is not only listed by the IUCN on its Red List and by CITES on Appendix I, which forbids international trade, but importantly, it is now also protected by Malagasy law.

Project Angonoka was started in 1986 to conduct research on the tortoise and to protect its environment using the help of local people. Baly Bay communities worked on conservation projects including creating firebreaks on the savanna fringes to prevent runaway fires. This was successful and helped enormously in reducing the effects of wildfires. As well as these activities, in 1986 a captive-breeding site was opened. Eight years later, the centre had produced 100 young tortoises, but disaster was to strike. In May 1996, 76 tortoises were stolen from the centre – two adult females and 74 young. Some time later, 33 tortoises were found for sale in the Netherlands. The centre continued its work, producing 224 captive-bred tortoises from 17 adults by December 2004. The thieves from 1996 have yet to be brought to justice.

POACHING PROBLEMS

There is a lack of enforcement regarding the exotic pet trade, which allows thieves to get away with their crimes. In Madagascar, conservationists are so concerned that they have begun engraving identifying marks into the shells of the tortoises in order to reduce their value on the market. They are careful not to engrave below the keratin layer, to avoid causing pain to the tortoise.

Market forces continue to drive up levels of poaching, and in March 2014 one tenth of the world population of Angonoka Tortoises was found in a smuggler's bag at Suvarnabhumi International Airport in Bangkok, Thailand. The bag contained 54 Angonoka Tortoises and 21 Radiated Tortoises – the latter being another Critically Endangered tortoise species that is endemic to Madagascar.

On 20 March 2016, 146 tortoises were taken by customs officials at Mumbai Airport, India, from the possession of a Nepali citizen. The consignment included 139 Radiated Tortoises and seven Angonoka Tortoises. And on 12 June the same year a breeding centre in Thailand found that six Angonoka Tortoises and 72 Radiated Tortoises had been stolen.

A SPECIES ON THE BRINK

Poaching is causing a serious deterioration in an already extremely fragile population. Prices commanded in the global pet trade are so high that they become a real incentive to poachers. Conservationists are working hard, but they are up against time pressures. It takes 20 years for a female Angonoka Tortoise to reach sexual maturity, but extinction is thought to be a distinct possibility in less than a generation.

The wild population is certainly on the decrease with an estimated 600 animals remaining, although that figure could vary from 440–770. Researchers estimate that the Angonoka Tortoise faces a strong likelihood of extinction in the wild in the next 10–15 years.

Hawksbill Turtle

Eretmochelys imbricata

KEY FACTS

» This turtle species has been in existence for more than 100 million years.

» Two subspecies are recognised – the Indo-Pacific Hawksbill Turtle and the Atlantic Hawksbill Turtle.

» Has a specialised diet of sponges that would be fatal to other organisms, thereby playing a vital role within the ecosystem of the coral reef.

» Unique as the only reptile species to exhibit biofluorescence.

» Its flesh has been documented as a delicacy since at least the 5th century BC, when it was eaten by the emperors in China. Its shell has been used since Egyptian times.

» Habitat degradation and hunting for its shell has caused an 80 per cent decrease in population over the past 100 years.

» The IUCN listed the Hawksbill Turtle as Endangered in 1982 and changed its status to Critically Endangered in 1996.

CHARACTERISTICS AND STATUS

The Hawksbill Turtle is found in oceans around the world, predominately in places with deep water where there are plenty of coral reefs with abundant supplies of their food. Two subspecies are recognised, the Indo-Pacific Hawksbill Turtle (*E. i. bissa*) and the Atlantic Hawksbill Turtle (*E. i. imbricata*).

The species is like any other sea turtle in that it has a relatively flattened body-shape contained within a toughened shell or carapace, with arms and legs designed to help it swim in the strong currents of the sea. It is small to medium-sized, with an adult measuring an average of 1m (3ft) in length and weighing 80kg (180lb). Its shell has eye-catching radiating streaks which give it a zigzag effect due to its overlapping scales. The flipper-like arms and legs are clawed. Females have smaller claws and a duller tail than males. An individual will typically live for 30–50 years.

The Hawksbill Turtle differs from other turtles due to its curved knife-like bill-tip, with a V-shaped jawbone which is adapted for uprooting sponges from cracks in the reef. It also has two pairs of prefrontal scales, heavy dorsal overlapping scutes on the carapace, four sets of costal scutes and two pinchers on each flipper. The flanks and back end of the shell are highly jagged in all but the very oldest of these reptiles. Another difference between this species and other sea turtles is its deportment on land – although turtles all have a uniform movement when traversing sand, it is only the Hawksbill that will leave asymmetrical trails.

Hawksbill Turtles spend a lot of time feeding among corals and in shallow lagoons, but otherwise live out in the open ocean. The IUCN has classified the species as Critically Endangered, in part due to high levels of bycatch from harmful fishing practices, although it is also deliberately hunted for its shell and other products, even though this is outlawed by the Convention of International Trade in Endangered Species (CITES).

CARVING OUT A DIETARY NICHE

The adult Hawksbill Turtle predominately eats sponges (70–95 per cent of its diet), but will also feed on comb jellies as well as jellyfish, molluscs, sea urchins, algae, sea anemones, fish and crustaceans. It will also prey upon cnidarians such as the stinging Portuguese Man O' War (*Physalia physalis*), shutting its eyes for protection while eating. The turtle's armoured shell screens its head and helps to prevent any danger. It has a specialised diet of sponges that would be fatal to other organisms, thereby playing a vital role within the ecosystem of the coral reef. The flesh of the Hawksbill Turtle can become highly toxic to predators due to its diet.

They also eat the biofluorescent coral *Physogyra lichtensteini*, which has recently been shown to give the turtle biofluorescence – a trait that is unique among reptiles.

This species has been in existence for more than 100 million years and during this time it has carved out its own unique niche in the ecosystem, playing a vital role in conserving the health of coral reefs and sea grass beds.

Nesting

The Hawksbill Turtle uses many of the same nesting beaches as the Green Turtle, often beside isolated lagoons in places with vegetation to hide the nest. Atlantic populations tend to breed between April and November and Indian Ocean populations between September and February. Nests have been located in 60 countries, with high densities in places such as Australia, Mexico, the Seychelles and Indonesia.

Females come ashore at night to dig a hole with their anterior flippers. They will lay a clutch of around 140 eggs and conceal the hole with sand before making their way back to sea. A female will lay eggs approximately four or five times per breeding season, with a period of about 15 days between each deposition, and will tend to use the same nesting sites time and time again.

Hatchlings

The eggs take 60 days to hatch. It is not known whether the gender of the hatchlings is related to temperature – a trait found in other turtles and reptiles.

The babies hatch at night and use the light of the moon to direct them to the sea. When human development occurs close to nesting beaches, the baby turtles can easily become disorientated by street lighting and lights from buildings and make their way towards them instead of the ocean, making them easy prey for birds, crabs and other predators. The nest itself is prone to attack from small mammals.

Predators and threats

Natural predators of the Hawksbill Turtle include sharks, crocodiles, octopuses and large fish. However their greatest hazard lies in human activity such as fishing. The flesh of the Hawksbill Turtle has been documented as a delicacy from the 5th century BC, when it was eaten by emperors in China.

TRADE IN TORTOISESHELL

The substantial and beautiful shell that defends the turtle in its ecosystem is what is most highly prized by humans. The shell has been used since Egyptian times, with the Ancient Greeks and Romans making jewellery from it and historical use in Japan for producing musical instruments.

Nowadays the sale of the tortoiseshell is pronounced in places such as Colombia, the Dominican Republic and other countries in the Caribbean, while Japan imports 30,000kg (66,000lb) every year. Countries have signed up to CITES, but many, such as Japan and Cuba, have exempted themselves with regard to the Hawksbill Turtle. Other countries signed up to CITES, such as Indonesia, disregard the agreement when it comes to the Hawksbill Turtle, while countries such as Haiti have not signed CITES at all.

THREATS AND HABITAT DEGRADATION

Historically, habitat degradation has caused an 80 per cent decrease in the Hawksbill Turtle population over the past 100 years. The IUCN registered the species as Endangered in 1982, but because there was not a population increase, by 1996 it changed its status to Critically Endangered.

Although the Hawksbill Turtle is threatened by loss of nesting sites and feeding locations, egg foraging, fishing bycatch, pollution and coastal development, its biggest danger lies in the wildlife trade. The species has extremely slow reproductive rates, which means that populations take an enormously long time to recover from any losses sustained.

Leatherback Turtle

Dermochelys coriacea

KEY FACTS

» Biggest sea turtle in existence. Its clawless flippers can reach 2.7m (8.9ft) in length.

» Has the greatest range of any sea turtle, extending from the Cape of Good Hope in Africa to the polar seas around the Arctic Circle.

» Can dive to depths of 1,280m (4,200ft) and feeds on twice its own bodyweight in jellyfish in each day.

» Often mistakenly feeds on plastic bags thinking they are jellyfish, with dire health consequences.

» Its eggs are considered a delicacy in various regions of the world and collected in thousands. As a result it has declined in many countries and become extinct in Malaysia.

» Pacific populations have diminished by 90 per cent in the past 20 years.

LAST OF ITS KIND

The Leatherback Turtle is the biggest sea turtle in existence. Its evolutionary history can be traced back to the first evolved turtles of the Cretaceous Period, some 115 million years ago. It has great mass for a reptile, with only three crocodile species weighing more than it. It differs from other turtles in that it lacks a keratin shell – instead its carapace is formed of oily skin.

The Leatherback has a hydrodynamic, comma-shaped body. It pushes through the water with enormous, clawless flippers that can reach 2.7m (8.9ft) in length. Body length is on average 1–1.75m (3.3–5.7ft), giving the animal a total length of 1.83–2.2m (6.0–7.2ft). Weight is in the region of 250–700kg (550–1,540lb). Hatchlings have a body length of 6.1cm (2.4in) and weigh 46g (1.6oz) at the point of emergence.

Experts are divided on the lifespan of the Leatherback Turtle. Some say 30 years, others 50, although we are fairly certain that is not more than 100 years. When they die they provide a rich microecosystem to nourish other organisms. They are an important link in the marine ecosystem.

EVOLUTION TO SURVIVE IN FREEZING WATERS

This turtle has evolved so that it is able to maintain a body temperature 18°C (32°F) greater than the water in which it is swimming, which is especially relevant for cold subpolar waters. This is achieved by using a combination of methods. The first is the fatty adipose tissue that forms a large part of the animal's body mass – this can maintain the body's temperature even in cold seas. The second is their large flippers which act as heat exchangers to the body, keeping it warm whatever the temperature. Also, the body is able to create heat through movement and since the Leatherback Turtle only spends 0.1 per cent of the day at rest, its continuous activity could be a significant factor in generating body heat.

BREAKING RECORDS

As well as being the biggest turtle, the Leatherback also has the greatest geographical range. This stretches far to the south, encompassing the Cape of Good Hope in South Africa and the southern waters of New Zealand, while at its northernmost boundaries it reaches Alaska and Norway, even inhabiting the waters of the polar seas around the Arctic Circle.

The Leatherback Turtle entered the *Guinness Book of Records* in 1992 when its maximum speed in the water was measured at 35.28kph (21.92mph). A more typical pace is 1.80–10.08kph (1.12–6.26mph).

Leatherbacks are also known for their deep dives, achieving depths of 1,280m (4,200ft). Depths such as these are only matched by beaked whales, sperm whales and elephant seals. The duration of one of their dives is typically 3–8 minutes, although dive times of 30–70 minutes have been recorded.

BREEDING HABITS AND DECLINE

Young turtles linger in the tropical and subtropical seas close to their nesting sites. Adults traverse the Atlantic and Pacific Oceans following traditional migratory routes and travel a long way in order to feast on jellyfish that inhabit cold waters. Males spend their entire life in the water and females only leave it in order to lay eggs.

Mating is by internal fertilisation. The female gives off a pheromone to tell the male that she is ready. He will nudge and nibble her to see if she is willing. A female will mate every 2–3 years, usually with numerous males, while the males mate annually.

Research shows that between 26,000–43,000 females lay eggs each year. This is a remarkable decline from studies in 1980 that suggested 116,000 nesting females.

JELLYFISH DIET AND PLASTIC BAG PERIL

The Leatherback Turtle loves to feed on jellyfish and plays an important role in regulating their numbers in the oceans. In a single day a Leatherback will feed on twice its own bodyweight in jellyfish. The great danger nowadays is the number of plastic bags in the oceans. Research indicates that one third of all turtles have swallowed plastic. It is worse in built up areas, such as San Francisco Bay and the Columbia River mouth. The turtles miscalculate plastic bags for jellyfish. It gets caught in their gut, displacing real food which has implications for growth and development. It is believed that sexual maturation is affected, which has serious implications for breeding.

NATURAL PREDATION

Birds such as gulls and plovers will feast on Leatherback Turtle eggs. The young turtles are heavily predated by the likes of coyotes, mongooses, monitor lizards, raccoons, dogs, ghost crabs and genets. That peril continues on their journey to the sea, with added danger from frigatebirds and raptors. On reaching the ocean they face predation by requiem sharks and various large fish.

As an adult, life becomes slightly less fraught, even though they don't have a tough shell for protection. In the ocean, Orcas, Great White Sharks, Tiger Sharks and other large predators will kill a Leatherback Turtle. Nesting females are vulnerable to attack from Jaguars.

THREATS FROM HUMANS

Humans are much more of a cause for concern than any natural predator in terms of the scale of the damage that they can inflict on the species. Leatherback Turtle eggs are considered a delicacy in various regions of the world, and their collection at unsustainable levels has resulted in a total breakdown in Leatherback Turtle breeding in South-East Asia. The eggs are collected in their thousands, leading to complete extinction in Malaysia and significant reductions in populations elsewhere.

In the Caribbean, the eggs are thought to be an aphrodisiac. Apart from a small number of subsistence fishermen who eat the meat of adult turtles, their flesh is generally judged to be too fatty and oily to enjoy.

Rising sea-levels are destroying breeding sites, while land clearance creates sedimentation which, together with agricultural run-off of nutrients, can cause serious pollution problems. Artificial lighting from huge coastal developments confuses new hatchlings when they are trying to make their way to the sea. They usually follow the light of the moon, but streetlights and car headlights can cause them to travel in the wrong direction, often leading to danger.

Leatherbacks are frequently caught as bycatch when fishing, and it is very difficult to untangle them from nets due to their large size. It is believed that 1,500 are caught in this way every year in the Pacific alone.

The fishing industry is ever increasing in scale and frequently adopting unsustainable practices, while plastic waste and chemical pollution in the seas are often causes of turtle death. The Pacific population of Leatherback Turtles has diminished by 90 per cent in the previous 20 years and declines have been noted elsewhere.

TAKING STEPS TO SAVE LEATHERBACKS

Turtles have been tagged so that their movements across the oceans can be tracked in order to ensure that interplay with fishing boats can be kept to a minimum, and also to help locate favoured nesting sites and feeding grounds.

Conservationists are training rangers to patrol beaches and work with local communities to initiate ecotourism, which generates an income source.

The beaches of Mayumba, Gabon, provide nesting grounds for thousands of female Leatherbacks between September and April each year. The beaches

of this small town, with a population of 2,500 people, have been afforded national park status, and this has been significant in attracting ecotourism. This is in stark contrast to the plight of nesting female Leatherbacks in Brazil, which attracts an average of only seven turtles each year. The Brazilian government is working with fishermen to stop bycatch and to safeguard nests.

California Condor

Gymnogyps californianus

KEY FACTS

» At 3.0m (9.8ft), it has the greatest wingspan of all North American birds.

» One of the world's largest flying birds, with a life expectancy of 60 years.

» Can fly at speeds of 90kph (56mph) and heights of 4,600m (15,100ft).

» Declared extinct in the wild in 1987, when the remnant population of 27 birds was taken into captivity.

» They are still one of the world's rarest birds but in December 2016 there were 446 condors alive, either in the wild or captivity.

HISTORY

The biggest North American landbird and one of the largest flying birds in the world, California Condors were once kept as pets during the Californian Gold Rush. The species was declared extinct in the wild in 1987, when the remnant population of 27 birds was taken into captivity. It has since been sucessfully bred and reintroduced into areas in California, northern Arizona and southern Utah, where some birds fly over iconic locations such as the Grand Canyon and Zion National Park.

WINGSPAN AND WEIGHT

At 3.0m (9.8ft) the condor has the largest wingspan of all birds in North America and can weigh up to 12kg (26lb) – only the Trumpeter Swan is heavier. The male is larger than the female. They rank among the longest lived of all birds with a life expectancy of 60 years.

A STRIKING BIRD

Juveniles are brownish, with adult plumage attained at 6–8 years. Adults are mainly black with striking white patches on the underside of the wings and a frill of feathers around the hind neck. The bald head can communicate various emotions, flushing from yellowish to glowing red when a bird is excited or alarmed – juveniles do not have this capacity. Furthermore adults have a throat sack which enlarges during courtship.

FEEDING AND CLEANING

These birds are often thought of as dirty, as they are scavengers rather than predators, feeding on dead and rotting meat using their strong bills to rip through resilient hide. They play an important role in the ecosystem in terms of cleaning up the debris of life. Their heads get pretty messy when they are plunged neck-deep into a carcass, which is one very good reason that they have a bald head. After feeding they often use rocks, grass or branches to scrub up. They regularly bathe and while away the hours preening their feathers. Condors have a very strong and resilient immune system which protects them from potentially harmful bacteria.

BIENNIAL BREEDERS

The birds tend to pair for life. The female lays one greenish-white egg between January and April every two years. Both parents play a part in incubation, which takes 53–60 days. The chicks hatch with their eyes wide open and have an ashy down. They are competent flyers after 5–6 months, but stay with their parents near the nest until they are approaching two years old, when the parents begin the process once again.

HABITAT

Rocky shrubland, coniferous forests and oak savannahs are typical habitats for the condor. They nest in high-up places which facilitate an easy take-off. Cliffs, caves and enormous tree cavities – such as those of the giant sequoia or redwood – provide perfect nesting sites at elevations of up to 1,800m (6,000ft). The range of these magnificent birds formerly covered wide areas from Canada to Mexico, from the Pacific coast to the Atlantic coast, with fossil records to prove it. An individual will journey up to 250km (160 miles) in search of carrion.

FLIGHT

The arrangement of the condor's wings and positioning of its feathers are perfect for enabling these enormous birds to soar. They rarely flap their wings and are extraordinarily graceful in flight. To take off they will beat their wings, but after achieving a slight elevation they are able to glide using thermals, so that they can travel long distances with barely a flap of the wings. They are capable of reaching speeds of up to 90kph (56 mph) and heights of up to 4,600m (15,100ft).

A CARRION SPECIALIST

Historically California Condors would feed on the carcasses of dead antelope, elk and other big animals. However, by the late 1900s prey numbers fell and the population of condors was restricted to the mountainous areas in southern California where dead sheep, cattle and deer became the staple diet. They tend to avoid bird and reptile remains, but goats, donkeys, horses, pigs, cougars and bears are favourites. They will also eat smaller mammals such as rodents, rabbits or coyotes, and feast on the carcasses of marine animals such as sea lions, whales and salmon.

POWERFUL EYESIGHT, SMALL CLAWS

Condors do not have a terrific sense of smell, but they have powerful eyesight which enables them to see carcasses from a distance. They will also watch for other scavengers such as eagles or smaller vultures, who will lead them to a meal. A Golden Eagle will challenge a condor over a carcass, but otherwise the condor will threaten other avian foragers away. A condor eats every few days, but can go for two weeks without dining. They will demolish 1–1.5kg (2.2–3.3lb) of meat in one sitting.

The condor's claws are not adapted to gripping as they lack the talons that eagles or hawks have. Instead they have unsharpened claws, more adapted to walking. They are unable to clench or move prey as they do not have a toe that faces to the rear.

SOCIAL LIFE

Condors are very social birds, gathering at roosts, bathing grounds and carcasses. They have a strong social hierarchy, with dominant birds feeding first. They use body language, combative play and vocal sounds to decide social status. Condors lack a true voice box that is present in other birds, so they can only make unrefined basic grunts or hisses. Chicks make a high-pitched shriek to gain attention from their parents.

THREATS

Lead poisoning, DDT poisoning, electric power lines, egg collecting and habitat destruction have caused 60 per cent of adult and juvenile mortalities in the wild. The leading cause of death in nestling condors is the devouring of rubbish that their parents have brought to feed them. It has been illegal to kill a California Condor for nearly 100 years.

CONSERVATION

Throughout the 20th century, poaching, lead poisoning and habitat degradation led to a rapid decrease in Californian Condor numbers, which caused the US government to act. They trapped all the remaining birds as part of a conservation plan, completing the work on Easter Sunday 1987. As a result they had a captive population of 27 condors which they bred at Los Angeles Zoo and San Diego Wild Animal Park. This project proved so successful that by 1991 they were able to release condors back into the wild. The California Condor is still one of the world's rarest birds but it is showing an upward trend, and by December 2016 there were 446 alive, either in the wild or in captivity.

Philippine Eagle

Pithecophaga jefferyi

KEY FACTS

» The world's largest eagle in terms of length.

» Nests 30m (99ft) above the ground in a structure 1.5m (4.9ft) in diameter.

» Life expectancy 30–60 years. Birds in captivity live longer and grow larger.

» Only 220 birds remain in the wild. The species has been close to extinction for the past 40 years.

» There is a prison sentence of up to 12 years for killing this eagle.

» Captive breeding has been successful.

» Only 9,220km^2 (3,560 miles^2) of its old-growth forest habitat remains – 80 per cent of the rainforest has been destroyed since the 1970s due to expanding agriculture and logging.

ONE OF A KIND

The Philippine Eagle is also known as the Monkey-eating Eagle. It was first formally described for science in 1894 and today is found on only four islands – Mindanao, Luzon, Leyte and Samar – with the greatest population on Mindanao.

It is among the tallest, most unusual and strongest birds alive today. DNA analysis shows it to have a unique evolutionary history with no recognised subspecies. It is probably most closely related to the much smaller snake eagles. Although it is not genetically similar to species like the Harpy Eagle, Crested Eagle and the New Guinea Harpy Eagle, convergent evolution has meant that these birds of prey are all of similar sizes and with comparable habits and habitats.

The species lives in the rainforests of the Philippines, ranging from the lowlands to mountains of over 1,800m (5,900ft). It has been close to extinction for the past 40 years as only 9,220km² (3,560 miles²) of its old-growth forest habitat still exists. The population is now feared to be less than 250 birds.

A FORMIDABLE PREDATOR

The Philippine Eagle's plumage is mostly brown above and white below with a shaggy, lion-like crest on the top and back of the head. It has heavy, yellowish legs with large, powerful claws, while the bluish bill is predominant and deep. The piercing blue eyes add to the impression of a formidable predator.

Chicks are white and juveniles are similar to their parents but with paler fringes to the feathers on the upperparts, while the legs are more yellow compared to those of the adult. Adults make long, piercing high-pitched whistles with inflections in pitch towards the end. Juveniles make a sequence of high-pitched calls when begging for food.

It is the world's largest eagle in terms of length, measuring 86–102cm (2.82–3.35ft). Birds kept in captivity tend to grow larger due to greater food availability. The eagles exhibit sexual dimorphism, with the males being 10–20 per cent smaller than the females. The female weighs around 7kg (15.5lb) and the male about 5kg (11lb). On average the wingspan is in the region of

2m (6.6ft), but it can be larger. A wild Philippine Eagle's life expectancy is 30–60 years, but birds in captivity live longer.

HUNTING IN THE RAINFOREST

The Philippine Eagle's flight is more similar to that of hawks rather than other large birds of prey as it is swift and nimble, using speed and agility to navigate its way through the dense forest. It is the apex predator in its territory.

The bird hunts by using two methods. The first is to sit and wait silently on a branch watching for prey. The second is to glide periodically down through the canopy, branch by branch, before swooping back up to the top again. Pairs of eagles can also hunt monkeys co-operatively with one bird watching the monkey troop and distracting them, only for its partner to swoop in from the rear for the kill. The macaques it feeds on are about the same size as the eagle, with an adult male weighing 9kg (20lb), and it has been known for an eagle to break a leg when struggling with this prey.

PREY SPECIES

The Philippine Eagle's prey varies according to location, particularly between the islands of Mindanao and Luzon which are in different faunal regions. For example flying lemurs, which are the primary food source in Mindanao, are not present on Luzon. On Luzon the eagle will eat monkeys, birds, flying foxes, reptiles (lizards and large snakes) and giant cloud rats. There are also records of of these eagles preying on young pigs, goats and small dogs. The Philippine Eagle has no predators apart from humans.

A SLOW BREEDER

The male Philippine Eagle reaches sexual maturity at the age of seven years, while the female is ready to reproduce at five years old. The breeding cycle lasts for two years. Similar to most eagles, the breeding pairs are monogamous and will stay together for life. Nest-building heralds the start of courtship, together with an aerial display where the male will chase the female and present his talons to her back during a diagonal dive. She will then turn in mid-air and present her own talons to him. Bringing nesting material to build the nest shows that they are ready to breed.

A pair of eagles will generally choose one of the tallest trees in their territory in which to build their nest. The nest is a huge platform of sticks, built 30m (99ft) above the ground. It is lined with green leaves and is 1.5m (4.9ft) in diameter. The same nest can be reused to raise several chicks over a period of years.

A pair of eagles requires a range of 65–130km² (25–50 miles²) in order to support their chick. The single egg is laid between October and December and birds on Mindanao and Luzon will breed at separate ends of this range. Rainfall and prey populations will affect the timing of the breeding season.

The eagles will typically incubate for 62 days and the female does the majority of the work, although the male will help. The eagle pair will mate again a few days after the egg has been laid in order to safeguard their breeding potential. The chick fledges after 4–5 months, although parental care continues from both parents for 20 months. This means that the eagle can only breed every two years, unless there has been a failed attempt. This, along with that of the California Condor, Crowned Eagle and Harpy Eagle, is the longest known breeding cycle in birds of prey.

RAISING AWARENESS

In 1978 there was a Presidential proclamation to change the eagle's name from the Monkey-eating Eagle to the Philippine Eagle. In order to increase awareness of the bird's plight, President Fidel V. Ramos declared the Philippine Eagle the country's National Bird on 4 July 1995. Heavy fines and a prison sentence of up to 12 years are in place in Philippine Law for anyone found killing this bird.

The eagle has also been depicted on 12 Filipino postage stamps between 1967–2007, while the 50-centavo coins produced between 1981–1994 also showed the eagle.

THREATS

In 2008, there were thought to be between 180–500 eagles left in the wild. Reduction of territory equates to a decline in prey animals and loss of the large nesting trees needed for breeding. Estimates suggest that 80 per cent of Filipino rainforests have disappeared since the 1970s. This prompted the IUCN to list the eagle as Critically Endangered in 2008.

In 2015, the wild population was estimated to be around 220. The eagle's habitat of old-growth forest continues to be lost at an alarming rate due to expanding agriculture and logging. Indeed, logging companies own most of the lowland forest.

Other threats such as mining, pollution, exposure to pesticides and poaching also make life difficult for the eagle. They are sometimes caught in traps set for deer, or collide with overhead power lines. As the eagle is at the top of the food chain, accumulation of pesticides in its prey species, which build up in the food chain, can present a real threat to the bird and its breeding success. Mud slides and flooding due to deforestation have caused havoc in the birds' territories. The eagle used to be caught for international trade to zoos, although this is no longer a problem as CITES has controlled the movement and trade of this species. However, birds are still occasionally hunted for food.

CAPTIVE BREEDING AND RELEASE

The first Philippine Eagle bred through artificial insemination hatched in 1992. The first eaglet bred through natural methods hatched in 1999. In 2004, in Mindanao, the first captive-bred eagle was released into the wild. This bird was accidentally electrocuted in January the following year. Another was released in March 2008, but a farmer shot it for food. Another tragic tale occurred in June 2015, when an eagle that had been treated for gunshot wounds was released only to be shot dead two months later. The legal protection that has been offered to this bird had helped to reduce the frequency of such incidents.

CONSERVATION

As a bare minimum, selective logging needs to be put into practice so that large nesting trees are protected and tracts of undisturbed forest left intact so that the birds can eat and support themselves. Further research is being undertaken to look at distribution, population size, ecological requirements and threats to the eagles, as well as understanding the socio-economic factors surrounding the birds.

Captive breeding has been successful. The Philippine Eagle Foundation is home to 36 birds, 19 of which were bred in captivity. Success in rewilding these birds is a key issue. There are protected areas, such as the 700km² (170,000 acres) of Cabuaya Forest and the 37.2km² (9,200 acres) of Taft Forest Wildlife Sanctuary on Samar, but there are key populations of Philippine Eagles on unprotected land.

Northern Bald Ibis

Geronticus eremita

KEY FACTS

» Formerly occurred widely across Central Europe, North Africa and the Middle East.

» Inhabits arid, barren, semi-desert conditions.

» Became the world's first officially protected species thanks to a decree from Archbishop Leonhard of Salzburg in 1504.

» Extinct in Europe for at least 300 years, while the last wild birds in the Middle East, which were breeding in Syria, died out during the past decade.

» West coast of Morocco is the final stronghold for wild birds with about 500 remaining, including 122 breeding pairs in 2017.

» Captive-bred birds are being reintroduced to Austria, Spain, Morocco and Turkey.

An unusual ibis

Unusually for members of its family, the Northern Bald Ibis does not wade in water, but instead feeds on insects, lizards and other small animals in low scrub and semi-desert. The birds are very social. Populations in Morocco are sedentary, while those formerly breeding in the Middle East were migratory, wintering south to Ethiopia. They breed on coastal or mountain cliffs, building a nest made of sticks and laying 2–4 eggs.

The genus name *Geronticus* comes from the Ancient Greek interpretation for 'old man', describing the bird's bald head. *Eremita* comes from the Latin word for 'hermit', denoting the remote environments which the bird occupies.

An unconventional beauty

The Northern Bald Ibis has long legs and a lengthy decurved bill. On average the bird measures 75cm (30in) from the tip of the bill to the tip of the tail and has a wingspan of 125–135cm (49–53in).

The plumage is completely black with glowing hints of iridescent blue, green, purple and copper when it catches the light. There is a shaggy ruff of feathers at the base of the neck, while the bare head, legs and long bill are all red.

The ibis is mostly silent, but during courtship and breeding it will hiss and grunt. There is no noticeable sexual dimorphism, although the males are slightly larger and have longer bills. Research suggests that males with longer bills are more successful at finding a mate.

HISTORICAL RANGE

Analysis of fossil remains found on the Mediterranean coast of Spain shows that the ancestors of the Northern Bald Ibis have been in existence for at least 1.8 million years. Historically the species was found across Central Europe, North Africa and the Middle East.

In Ancient Egypt, the Northern Bald Ibis was revered as a sacred bird, representing vividness and richness. It was thought to be a reincarnation of Thoth, who was scribe of the Gods, depicted by the body of a man and the head of an ibis, symbolising fruitfulness and purity. This ibis has religious significance in Turkey, which some suggest contributed to the persistence of a population in that region. It is believed that the bird was among the first that Noah freed from the Ark, conveying fruitfulness.

In Europe nesting sites were situated along the Rhone and Danube rivers and in the mountain ranges of Switzerland, Germany, Austria, Italy and Spain. Castle towers and turrets were documented as being used as nest sites by breeding pairs. In 1504, Archbishop Leonhard of Salzburg detected a decline in numbers and issued a decree making the Northern Bald Ibis the world's first officially protected species. However, despite his efforts the ibis became extinct in Europe more than 300 years ago.

MATES FOR LIFE

Sexual maturity is reached at the age of five and birds will pair for life. The male instigates the action by picking a nesting location, cleaning it and then attracting a female by shaking his chest and giving a low call. The bond between the pair is strengthened by reciprocal preening and nodding demonstrations.

Incubation time is 24–25 days. Subsequent feeding of the chicks is performed by both parents and the chicks fledge in a further 50 days. The expected lifespan of a Northern Bald Ibis is 10–15 years in the wild, while in captivity this inceases to 20–25 years.

RANGE AND DIET

During the breeding season the birds may forage in a territory with a radius of up to 15km (9.2 miles). Dry, steppe-like or semi-desert habitat is the preferred foraging ground, but they have been known to use fallow fields or even active agricultural fields. It is essential that vegetation is sporadic, and less than 15–20cm (5.9–7.9in) high.

If they can't find their favoured food of beetles and lizards they will also eat small mammals, ground-nesting birds and invertebrates such as caterpillars, spiders and snails. The long bill is adapted for probing soft surfaces and feeling for prey as the flock forages over a field.

NATURAL PREDATORS

The Common Raven is a predator of ibis eggs, but little is known regarding the predation of adult Northern Bald Ibises. In southern Africa its sister species, the Southern Bald Ibis (*Geronticus calvus*), is prone to attack from large raptors that use the same cliffs to breed. The primary hazard at chick-rearing sites is human disturbance during nesting and incubation and the predation of chicks by ravens.

A DRASTIC DECLINE

The decrease in numbers of the ibis has been pronounced for several centuries, being estimated at 98 per cent between 1900 and 2002. The west coast of Morocco is the species final stronghold and this population is thought to number 500 birds, including 122 breeding pairs in 2017. The last wild birds in the Middle East bred in Syria, close to Palmyra, migrating south to winter in Ethiopia, but this tiny remnant population is now extinct.

The population decline is due to several factors, including notable human mistreatment particularly in the form of uncontrolled hunting, the loss of steppe and non-intensive agricultural feeding grounds, disturbance at breeding sites and poisoning through the use of pesticides. However, the international conservation response has been good, with reintroduction schemes being initiated in Austria, Spain and northern Morocco, as well as a project involving semi-wild breeding birds at Birecik in Turkey.

CONSERVATION SUCCESS IN MOROCCO

One of the greatest achievements to date is that the wild population of Northern Bald Ibises in Morocco has at last turned a corner and begun to increase, reaching 100 breeding pairs in 2008 and 122 in 2017. This was all achieved through a series of simple but effective actions such as providing drinking water for the birds and making sure that predators and competitors are kept well away. Wardens have looked after valuable feeding grounds, and a combination of conservationists, governments, researchers, funders and individuals have facilitated this positive progress.

SEMI-WILD BIRDS IN TURKEY

With the wild population of ibises becoming extinct in Turkey, the government acted to initiate the foundation of a semi-wild population at Birecik. This has been a great success with 205 Northern Bald Ibises resident as of March 2016. The birds are released from captivity in January and February to breed predominantly on the ledges around the complex, while they hunt and feed in the nearby fields. In July and August the birds are recaptured before they can migrate. The aim is to permit some birds to migrate again once the population reaches 100 breeding pairs.

Siberian Crane

Leucogeranus leucogeranus

KEY FACTS

» The Siberian Crane underwent a steep decline during the 20th century, and as of 2010 the total population stood at 3,200 individuals.

» Of two remaining breeding populations, both in the Arctic tundra, the western one is on the brink of extinction, so today more than 99 per cent of the birds breed in eastern Russia and winter in China.

» Key Chinese wintering grounds in the Poyang Lake basin, which drains into the Yangtze River, have been badly affected by the construction of the Three Gorges Dam and other projects, with more hydrological schemes being proposed.

» The oldest Siberian Crane is known to have lived for 83 years.

» Captive breeding has been attempted, with artificial insemination tried after it was found that males had a tendency to kill their partner.

» Eggs from captive birds were hatched using floodlights to mimic the long daylight hours of the Arctic summer.

LAST OF THE 'SNOW CRANES'

The scientific name *Leucogeranus* comes from the Greek words *leukos* meaning 'white' and *geranos* meaning 'crane'. The bird also goes by the name of 'snow crane'. As these names suggest, its plumage is snowy white with the exception of the black primary feathers, which are only seen when the bird is airborne.

There were formerly two breeding populations, both on the Arctic tundra, but the one based to the south of the Ob River, to the east of the Ural Mountains on the western side of Russia, is effectively extinct, with just perhaps the odd bird or pair remaining. These birds formerly wintered in India, along the Caspian Sea coast of Iran, and even as far west as the Nile in Egypt.

The remaining birds breed far to the east, also in Russia, in north-eastern Siberia. They make a long journey south to China for the winter, where the bulk of the population gathers close to the Yangtze River. During migration the birds travel in pairs or in small groups of up to ten.

A LARGE AND STRIKING BIRD

The Siberian Crane measures about 140cm (55in) in length, with a mean weight of 4.9–8.6kg (11–19lb). The wingspan is in the range of 210–230cm (83–91in). Males and females are superficially similar, although the male is slightly larger and has a marginally longer bill. Their vocalisations differ markedly from those of other cranes, which tend to trumpet. Instead the Siberian Crane communicates with a high-pitched whistle.

Adults have a patch of bare red skin around the face, encompassing the forecrown, throat and sides of the head as far back as the eyes. The legs are also red and the bill dark. The adult's plumage is completely white with the exception of the black primaries.

Juveniles have feathered faces and a brown plumage. They are born with blue eyes, but these turn yellowish at the age of about six months.

AN UNUSUAL BILL

Unusually for a crane, the species has a serrated bill, which is useful when feeding in wetlands on submerged roots and tubers. It was originally thought that the serrated bill was an adaptation for eating fish, but studies have shown that the birds favour vegetation and will only take fish when plant matter is concealed by snow and ice still present in Russia from the winter months.

Although Siberian Cranes are omnivorous and able to eat anything their diet mainly includes roots, tubers, seeds and berries of plants such as hellebores, crowberries and cranberries, while rodents, fish, insects and earthworms are sometimes taken. Grit and pebbles are also ingested to aid food digestion.

Courtship behaviour

Like other cranes, once they are paired up, the male and female will take part in duetted calling, especially during the courtship season from May until June. An elaborate system of body language and high-pitched vocalisations make up the mating calls where both partners will stand with their heads thrown back and bills pointed skywards. The male will lift his wings behind his back while the female always keeps her wings by her side. There are distinct differences in calling between different pairs. Pairs will walk around other pairs showing them threatening behaviour. Cranes are also known to dance – jumping, running, bowing, wing-flapping and tossing sticks or grass. This is also a part of courtship, although not exclusively.

Nesting and fledging

Siberian Cranes migrate back to the Arctic tundra to breed at the end of April or beginning of May. The nest is constructed of grasses and sedges and situated in shallow water at the edge of a lake, with the pair making a flat mound standing 12–15cm (4.7–6in) proud of the waterline.

Two eggs are usually laid at the start of June, once the final snow has melted from the tundra, and the male protects them until they hatch after 27–29 days. One chick will usually die, due to the competitiveness between the two young birds, but the other will go on to fledge and make its first flight in around 80 days.

Falling numbers

Siberian Cranes have decreased in number during the 20th century. In 2010, the total population was estimated at 3,200 individuals. It doesn't help that the population of these cranes increases by less 10 per cent per annum after each breeding season, which is the smallest level of productivity in any species of crane.

Siberian Crane numbers have fallen due to factors such as hunting, adaptions in land use, habitat degradation, filtration of wetlands for reuse in farming, and other land-use changes along their migration routes. In addition their nests are prone to disturbance from Reindeer and Reindeer herders' dogs.

Siberian Cranes are very loyal to their wintering grounds. They inhabit the same places year after year. They are similar to other cranes in favouring shallow marshlands and wetlands but will feed in deeper water compared to other cranes.

SPECIALISED NEEDS

The Siberian Crane is the most complex member of the crane family with regard to habitat requirements, morphology, vocalisations and behaviour. They require wetlands for feeding, nesting and roosting to a greater extent than other cranes and will exhibit quite different behaviour to other members of the family. These specialisations make the Siberian Crane more vulnerable and as a result it is the most endangered out of the world's 15 crane species.

CAPTIVE BREEDING AND ARTIFICIAL INSEMINATION

Captive breeding of Siberian Cranes has been attempted but it was found that males had a tendency to kill their partner, so artificial insemination has been tried. This has been successful at the International Crane Foundation at Baraboo, USA, where the eggs were hatched using floodlights to mimic the long daylight hours of the Arctic summer.

PRESSURE FROM DEVELOPMENT

The Siberian Crane's wintering grounds and migratory routes are under pressure due to loss and degradation of habitat as a result of economic development, as well as the general increased demand for land from a rapidly increasing human population.

Hunting still occurs in Pakistan and Afghanistan, and that together with war in Afghanistan may have have an impact on the migration success of the last birds in the western population.

Key wintering grounds in the Poyang Lake basin, which drains into the Yangtze River in China, have been badly affected by the construction of the Three Gorges Dam and other hydrological projects.

Since 2001, nearly 1,000 new dams have been built on the five rivers which lead onto Poyang Lake, greatly impacting the hydrological pattern in the area. The number of Siberian Cranes is predicted to decline rapidly in the coming years as the Three Gorges Dam is extended to include many

other dams on the Yangtze River and its tributaries. Recently a dam has been proposed for the Poyang Lake where the cranes spend the winter, which would have a dramatic effect on their wellbeing.

The increasingly small population of cranes makes them very vulnerable to disease or extreme weather. Inbreeding is bound to occur, reducing their genetic diversity and therefore resistance to disease.

Pangolin

Manidae species

KEY FACTS

» 70 million insects are consumed by each pangolin every year, giving them a crucial role in the ecosystem.

» They have an elongated tongue which is often longer than their body – it starts near the pelvis and folds up in a sheath in the chest.

» Natural predators include leopards, lions and tigers. However, the pangolins' scales are too strong to bite through and they will often lash out ferociously with their tail.

» Pangolin meat is regarded as a delicacy in Africa, China and Vietnam.

» Pangolins roll up into a ball when threatened, which makes them very easy to pick up and poach.

» Although there is an international ban, the market in pangolin trading is thought to be worth nearly US$20 billion per annum.

» More than 1 million pangolins are known to have been traded in the past 10 years, equating to 20 per cent of all illegal wildlife trade, although the actual figure could be as high as 10 million pangolins during the 10 years.

» The pangolin is very close to extinction in many parts of Asia and traffickers are now focusing their attentions on Africa.

EXTINCT AND EXTANT SPECIES

The name 'pangolin', comes from the Malayan word *pengguling*, meaning 'something that rolls up'.

There are a number of extinct species of pangolin. The extant family Manidae comprises three genera: *Manis*, which has four species in Asia, and *Phataginus* and *Smutsia*, which both have two species living in Africa. Asian pangolins differ from their African relatives in that they have thick bristles in between each scale.

These animals are extensively hunted by humans for their meat and scales, but also are threatened by deforestation and habitat loss. Two species of pangolin are classified as Critically Endangered according to the IUCN. These are the Chinese Pangolin, *Manis pentadactyla*, and the Malayan Pangolin, *Manis javanica*. Two other species are listed as Endangered and the remaining four are Vulnerable.

LONG TONGUE, TOUGH SCALES

Pangolins range from 30–100cm (12–39in) in length and will inhabit tree hollows or burrows, depending on their species. They range from pale brown to dark brown and superficially resemble reptiles due to the large defensive keratin scales which cover their entire body – a feature that is unique among mammals. These sharp scales are very heavy, making up 20 per cent of the entire body mass of a pangolin, and overlap for added protection. King George III was given a coat of armour made exclusively from pangolin scales in 1820. Appropriately an alternative name for the pangolin is 'scaly anteater'.

The Long-tailed Pangolin, otherwise known as the African Black-bellied Pangolin, *Phataginus tetradactyla*, is the only species to venture out during daylight. The others emerge at night to hunt, using their exceptionally long tongues to feed on ants and termites. The tongue is up to 40cm (16in) long and often longer than the body, starting near the pelvis and folding up in a sheath in the sternum. Pangolins have an acute sense of smell, which aids them while out hunting. The three long curved claws on the front feet are useful for burrowing into termite mounds and have the added bonus of enabling the pangolin to climb.

Repelling predators

Natural predators of the pangolin include leopards, lions and tigers. If under attack the pangolin curls up like a hedgehog, with its tail covering its face and its underbelly secure. Its scales are too strong to bite through and the pangolin will often lash out with its ferocious tail, which can wound the predator. It also gives out a toxic-smelling liquid from glands around the anus, which can function as a protective measure and can also be used to establish authority and sexual status.

Arboreal and terrestrial pangolins

An arboreal pangolin will burrow in a tree-hollow, while a terrestrial pangolin will utilise its sharp claws to create pits up to 3.5m (11.5ft) deep. Pangolins will dig using their tails and back legs for stability, and their scales to quarry the roof and walls of the chamber. Some pangolins move on all fours, their front claws rolled up in a ball, while others can balance on their hind legs to walk. Tree-living pangolins sway from bough to branch with their tails – they use their sharp front claws to tear bark, revealing insect nests. Pangolins are also adept at swimming.

Pangolin habitat differs for each species, but all occupy land where ants and termites can be found, which can be in places as diverse as tropical and flooded forests, cleared and cultivated areas, thick brush and savannah grassland. In Asia pangolins suffer hugely from habitat destruction, which is being reused for agriculture and settlement.

Specialised diet

Pangolins are insectivores and have quite a specialised diet of ants and termites, although they will also feed on bee larvae, flies, worms and crickets. They often grow sickly in captivity when fed alien food. They can block their nostrils and shut their eyes when feeding to defend themselves against their prey, while they have muscular control in their mouths to prevent insects escaping. They require on average 140–200g (4.9–7.1oz) of food every day.

With roughly 70 million insects consumed by each pangolin every year, these animals play a crucial role in the ecosystem.

IMPORTANT SENSES

Scientists find it difficult to study pangolins as they are incredibly shy. What they do know is that they have a very bad sense of sight, with miniscule eyes in relation to their body size. As a result their senses of smell and hearing are paramount. Their long sticky tongues with specialised glands reach down into the termite mound. Since they have no teeth, they have to utilise small stones to aid digestion of the ants by grinding them down.

WOOING WITH DUNG

Pangolins are generally solitary creatures, but come together to mate. The mating season is variable, although autumn and summer tend to be the most popular times. Males will create a trail with urine and dung and the females will follow their scent. Males will fight over a female, thrashing their tails at their opponents. Generally males are 10–50 per cent heavier than females, although in some Indian species they can be 90 per cent heavier.

ARMOUR-LESS BABIES

The gestation period is 70–140 days, varying with each species. An African pangolin will produce one baby per litter, while an Asian pangolin produces 1–3 young. Babies are a tiny, measuring 15cm (5.9in) long and weighing 80–450g (2.8–15.9oz), with soft white scales that harden over time. The young stay close to their mother and are weaned at three months, by which time they will begin an adult diet. At two years old they reach sexually maturity and begin to fend for themselves.

ILLEGAL TRADE

Pangolin meat is treated as a delicacy in Africa, China and Vietnam. The animals parts also have medicinal uses, with the scales being used for palsy, starting lactation and the drainage of pus. More than 1 million pangolins were traded in the last ten years even though there is an international ban. This is considered to equate to 20 per cent of all illegal animal trade, even though this is thought to represent only 10 per cent of actual pangolin trade. It does not help that pangolins roll up in a ball when threatened, which makes them very easy to pick up and poach.

REHABILITATION IN CAPTIVITY

Pangolins rescued from the animal trade are rehabilitated in captivity. They tend to not respond well and often suffer from pneumonia and ulcers. Much of this disease is due to the stress of being captured and traded. Breeding in captivity has not produced many positive results due to the specialised feeding habits and habitats of the animal. In captivity, a pangolin has lived for a maximum of 19 years, but it is thought that they can live for a lot longer in the wild.

INCREASED THREAT IN AFRICA

Conservationists are calling for stronger law enforcement and the penalisation of pangolin traffickers. The pangolin is very close to extinction in Asia and now these traffickers are focusing on African populations of the animal. The illegal market in trading pangolins is thought to be worth US$20 billion per annum, with the cost of pangolin scales increasing ten-fold during the past five years.

Black Rhinoceros

Diceros bicornis

KEY FACTS

» The rhinoceros came into being during the Eocene Period, some 50 million years ago.

» In the early 1900s several hundred thousand Black Rhinos occupied Africa, but by 1993 only 2,475 remained.

» Their horns are made of extremely durable keratin – the same substance found in hair and fingernails.

» Rhino horns are worth a fortune on the black market.

» Poaching is now organised in a systematic way by a transnational criminal network, with huge sums of money changing hands.

Black or White?

The Black Rhinoceros, also known as the 'Hook-lipped Rhinoceros', historically had a range that extended throughout much of Sub-Saharan Africa excluding the Congo Basin. It thrives in tropical and subtropical grasslands, savannas, deserts and shrublands.

The Black Rhino is actually grey or brown, with its exact shade depending upon local soil types. It has a pointed lip rather than the square upper jaw of the other African species, the White Rhino. The word 'white' actually comes from the Afrikaans word *wyd*, which means 'wide', reflecting the shape of its mouth. The lip shape denotes that the Black Rhino is a browser, and it uses its pointed lip to pull down branches from trees, cutting them with a clean angled edge. In contrast the White Rhino is a grazer and is adapted to eating grass. The Black Rhino is shyer and more combative than the White Rhino.

SUBSPECIES AND ANCESTRY

The IUCN recognises five subspecies of the Black Rhino, two of which are extinct. The rhino and other ungulates (hooved animals) came into being during the Eocene period, some 50 million years ago. Recognisable ancestors of the White and Black Rhinos were living in Africa 10 million years ago. The species split around 4–5 million years ago, from which time the Black Rhino could be found living in southern and eastern Africa including what today are Botswana, Kenya, Malawi, Mozambique, Namibia, South Africa, Swaziland, Tanzania, Zambia and Zimbabwe.

HORN FACTS AND FIGURES

An adult Black Rhino is 1.4–1.8m (4.6–5.9ft) high at the shoulder and 3–3.75m (9.8–12.3ft) long, weighing in the region of 800–1,400kg (1,800–6,385lb) with males being larger than females.

They have two horns, with the front one longer and averaging 50cm (20in), although it can grow to 140cm (55in). Sometimes a third posterior horn grows. These horns are made of extremely durable keratin (the same substance as in hair and fingernails), although they have been known to break during fighting. Males fight with their horns while females use them to defend their calf. They are also handy for unearthing roots and breaking branches in order to feed.

Today rhino horns are worth a fortune on the black market. They are used in traditional medicine in China, Hong Kong, Singapore and Taiwan, while in Africa and the Middle East they are used as ornamental dagger holders.

COMMUNICATION AND FIGHTING

Rhinos have a very substantial layer of skin to stop cuts and grazes caused by thorns or grasses. Their skin is home to parasites, such as mites and ticks that are eaten by birds such as Cattle Egrets and oxpeckers. The avian visitors also help to alert the rhino of danger.

The rhino suffers from incredibly bad eyesight, and as a result methods such as scent-marking are used in order to communicate with other Black

Rhinos in the area. They spray urine over trees and bushes within their territory, and around communal areas such as water holes and dung heaps. Black Rhinos are equipped with ears that can rotate in all orientations. These are very sensitive and can pick up sound waves over a great distance.

Black Rhinos can survive for five days without drinking and will follow elephant trails in order to reach water. They also create their own trails when feeding. They are surprisingly fast, reaching speeds of 55kph (34mph) and can make rapid changes in direction, going through bush or scrub. They are known to be particularly aggressive, charging in an instant if a threat is sensed. They regularly fight each other as well, with these battles ultimately accounting for 50 per cent of natural deaths in males and 30 per cent in females.

A VORACIOUS HERBIVORE

The Black Rhino is a herbivorous browser, eating leafy plants, shoots, branches, fruit and thorny wood, with acacias being a particular speciality, although the diet encompasses 220 different plant species in total. They browse during the morning and evening, at times when the sun is not too hot, and spend the rest of the day laying in the shade, sleeping or wallowing in mud. The mud lowers their body temperature and creates a layer over the skin which repels parasites.

African Elephants and Black Rhinos sometimes compete for food, in which case the elephant will assert its dominance. The area of an individual rhino's home range depends upon the time of year and what food is at hand. Females tend to have a larger home range than males, especially when they have a calf, and the ranges of females will often overlap. Males tend to be solitary and often territorial. Home ranges can be as little as 2.6km² (1.0 miles²) or as large as 133km² (51 miles²) depending on the availability of food.

BREEDING AND LIFE EXPECTANCY

Breeding takes place all year round with rhino pairs spending up to 30 days together and mating a few times daily, with copulation itself taking half an hour to complete. The calf is born after a gestation period of 15–16 months and is able to walk after three days. It is weaned at two years, but will stay with its mother for up to three years, until a new calf is born. Females can produce their own young from 5–7 years, whilst it takes a male 10 years to reach sexual maturity. Without the threat of poaching a Black Rhino can expect to live 40–50 years in the wild.

Historic Populations and Poaching

In the early 1900s several hundred thousand Black Rhinos occupied Africa. This number fell to 70,000 by the 1960s as the Black Rhino was hunted by European settlers. Its population decreased further to just 10,000–15,000 individuals by 1981 as unrestrained poaching for their horns took place, and by 1993 only 2,475 Black Rhinos remained. Poaching is now organised systematically by a transnational criminal network, with a lot of money changing hands. Anti-poaching measures have also increased substantially so that by 2017 there were 5,042–5,455 Black Rhinos in the wild.

Anti-poaching measures

CITES Appendix I, stating that the international commercial trade of Black Rhino horn is illegal, has been in place since 1977. The largest importer of rhino horn, China, joined CITES on 8th April 1981. Reserves created for the rhino have to be protected by security guards carrying guns. There have been experiments with removing the horns from rhinos in order to discourage poaching, even though the horn plays an important role in rhino society and the protection of their young. This idea did not work as poaching still continued at the same rate and it proved very expensive. Another less expensive idea is to move some rhinos to Australia or the USA and start new populations.

War and conservation efforts

Other serious issues include political instability and war in many parts of Africa, including countries such as Sudan, Somalia, Rwanda and Angola, which causes havoc with conservation work. An increase in poverty provides serious incentive for poaching. In 2014, 1,215 rhinos were killed by poachers in South Africa – an increase of 21 per cent on 2013.

The WWF is creating a database using DNA analysis of rhino horn in order to locate where the horn came from, which will help criminal investigations. In Namibia, WWF is working in conjunction with the government to develop transmitters to monitor rhino movement and defend the animals from poachers. TRAFFIC, an international body monitoring wildlife trade, has worked with South Africa and Vietnam to strengthen ties and information sharing. The Black Rhino Range Expansion Project started in 2003, and since then seven new Black Rhino populations have been created on 15,000ha (37,000 acres) of land in South Africa. This involved translocating nearly 120 Black Rhinos, while more than 30 calves have been born to date as a result of the project.

A PERMIT TO KILL

In January 2014 an auction was held at Dallas Safari Club for a permit to shoot a Black Rhino in Namibia. US$350,000 was paid. Subsequently death threats were made to the individual who bought the permit, as well as other members of the club. The rhino in question had been singled out by the Namibian Ministry of Environment and Tourism as it was too old to breed and was threatening other younger rhinos. The money raised by the auction was allocated by the government to help anti-poaching undertakings in the country. Simon Stuart, chair of the IUCN Species Survival Commission, told BBC News "You've got to imagine an animal walking around with a gold horn; that's what you're looking at, that's the value and that's why you need incredibly high security."

Sumatran Elephant

Elephas maximus sumatranus

KEY FACTS

» The herd is led by the oldest female – the matriarch – and is made up of related females.

» These elephants can live for 55–70 years. A male is not ready to breed until 15–20 years old.

» To keep the group unified the elephants communicate with a subsonic sound that can be heard 5km (3.1 miles) away.

» The main threats facing the elephant are habitat loss and conflict with humans.

» A group of elephants can obliterate a year's crop overnight. Retaliation by humans takes the form of shooting, electrocuting or poisoning.

» More than 70 per cent of elephant habitat has been lost over the last 25 years. Tesso Nilo National Park can sustain one population of elephants, but all remaining forest is in pockets not large enough to support a population.

» Extinction is predicted within 10 years.

IMPENDING MAMMAL EXTINCTION

The Sumatran Elephant is a subspecies of Asian Elephant that is endemic to the island of Sumatra, Indonesia; other subspecies are the Indian Elephant, Sri Lankan Elephant and Borneo Elephant. It is part of a growing list of Critically Endangered mammals in Sumatra according to the IUCN Red List – these include the Sumatran Orangutan, Sumatran Rhinoceros and Sumatran Tiger.

The main threats facing the elephant are habitat loss and human-elephant conflict. More than 70 per cent of their habitat has been lost over the last 25 years – a period equavalent to just one elephant generation. In the 22 years between 1985 and 2007 the elephant population halved. Conservationists have estimated the species has 10 years until extinction.

ELEPHANT SOCIETY

A Sumatran Elephant herd will consist of 5–35 animals led by the oldest female, the matriarch. The herd is made up of related females and its number depends upon food availability. Males either live alone or in small bachelor groups.

Adults measure 1.7–2.6m (5.6–8.5ft) at the shoulder and weigh 5 tons. Males do not have long tusks and those of the female are hidden under the upper lip. They have leathery blackish or brown skin, run at speeds of 44kph (28 mph), and can live for 55–70 years or more in captivity. Their sole predators are humans and tigers. Tigers will prey on younger elephants. Poachers will kill the males for their tusks, which leaves an imbalance in the male:female ratio that affects breeding success.

A female will become sexually mature at 10–13 years, but a male takes longer to assert the social dominance needed to mate, and is not ready to breed until he is 15–20 years. Breeding normally takes place at the height of the rainy season. In a suitable habitat a female will give birth every 2.5–4 years. After a gestation period of 22 months the newborn calf will weigh 50–150kg (110–330lb). The calf initially suckles from its mother but can eat grass and foliage after a few months. Weaning is completed in 2–3 years.

A female baby will stay with her mother for life, enjoying an extremely close bond, but a male offspring will be herded to the edge of the group as he becomes increasingly boisterous from the beginning of puberty aged 12. Eventually he will be forced out and begin his life as a solitary bull elephant.

A LARGE APPETITE

Sumatran Elephants spend more than two-thirds of their day eating. They consume up to 200kg (440lb) of food daily, which is equivalent to 5–10 per cent of their own body mass and roughly the weight of two and a half adult men. They will eat mainly grasses, but also an array of other plant matter including bark, roots, bananas, ginger, young bamboo, stems and the leaves of several vines. They are also partial to agricultural crops such as sugar cane, palm oil and rice.

Since Sumatra has a rich network of rivers the elephants are always near a water supply, which is just as well as they need to drink 80–200 litres (17.6–44 gallons) of water every day. One trunk-load amounts to 9 litres (2 gallons).

The elephants will bathe and wallow in the rivers, cooling down and using the mud to protect their skin from ectoparasite insects. Elephants can traverse deep rivers by holding their trunk up high and using it to breathe. If they are not close to a river they are able to dig 50–100cm (20–40in) into the soil with their front feet and trunk in search of water.

Elephant habitat includes swamp grassland, primary and secondary swamp forest, peat swamp forest, lowland forest 0–750m (0–2,460ft) above sea-level, and lower mountain rainforest 750–1,500m (2,460–4,920ft) above sea-level. They take refuge from the hot midday sun in dense vegetation. Elephants can cover 7km (4.4 miles) during the night and 15km (9.3 miles) per day over the fruiting or dry season. They follow permanent paths that are used year-round. Problems have occurred as farms have arisen along these well-trodden pathways with the elephants creating a large amount of devastation. While moving the elephants communicate to keep the group unified, using subsonic calls that can be heard 5km (3.1 miles) away.

A STEEP DECLINE IN POPULATION

A 1985 survey found 44 populations of Sumatran Elephant, containing 2,800–4,800 individuals. This included 12 populations in Lampung Province, but by 2002 just three of these groups remained. Dung density tests revealed that two of these populations were made up of 500 and 180 elephants. The third group was considered too small to be sustainable. The biological definition for population is a community of animals among whose members interbreeding occurs.

By 2008 numbers had further declined, leaving an estimated 350 individuals over nine groups. Numbers were considered too low to maintain long-term breeding success. In 2012 the Sumatran Elephant was declared Critically Endangered by the IUCN because of a 50 per cent decline during the course of one elephant generation of 25 years. With 85 per cent of the elephants' range existing beyond protected areas and with the dramatic increase in the oil-palm industry in Sumatra, human-elephant conflict is accelerating, resulting in a continuing rapid decline of elephant numbers. The Sumatran Elephant is considered likely to be extinct in 10 years.

TRANSMIGRATION AND INDUSTRY

The increase in industry in Sumatra comes as a result of large-scale transmigration within the Indonesian islands – for example 4.8 million people migrated to Sumatra in 1989 alone. People in densely populated islands such as Bali, Lombok, Madura and Java were dispersed to islands with less people, including Sulawesi, Borneo, Irian Jaya and Sumatra. This has resulted in some of the most colossal deforestation in the world, as lowland rainforests, rich in biodiversity, have been categorically destroyed in favour of logging, oil palm, pulpwood, paper and rubber. All forests have been ear-marked for logging, while it is only swamp ground and steep slopes that remain untouched. Elephants do not understand this, so massive conflict has arisen – a group of elephants can obliterate a year's crop overnight. Elephants can destroy homes and sometimes wound or even kill people. Retaliation by humans takes the form of shooting, electrocuting or poisoning.

ELEPHANT TRAINING CENTRES

The policy of the government during the period 1986–1995 was to capture the elephants that were causing the most problems and take them to Elephant Training Centres where they were trained to work in the forestry industry, nature conservation initiatives or ecotourism endeavours. This proved to be a very costly exercise and not good for the elephants. Around 700 were initially captured and the majority died in squalid conditions. The rest were dispatched to zoos and safari parks.

DIFFERENT CONSERVATION STRATEGIES

The year 2000 heralded a different tactic. The government decided to focus on conservation of the elephants and started to look after them a little better. The remaining captive animals received the medical attention that they deserved. They were used as vehicles during forest patrols and to push back crop-raiding elephants in order to prevent conflicts. This change in policy was only marginally successful and 100 wild elephants and 42 people still lost their lives between 2002–2007. Breeding is not considered an option with such a small population of only 400 captive elephants, and human-elephant conflict could result in the elephant dying out in the very near future.

THE TESSO NILO NATIONAL PARK AND REMAINING FOREST HABITAT

Conservation efforts continued however, with the Sumatran Elephant now protected under Indonesian law. The Tesso Nilo National Park was established in 2004 and can sustain one population of elephants. Remaining forest pockets elsewhere in Sumatra are all less than 250km² (96.5 miles²), which is not large enough to support an elephant population. However, the government is trying to create wildlife corridors between these patches of land, with the eventual aim of restoring the forest.

We are left with the grim reality that 85 per cent of elephant habitat is situated outside protected zones, and the likelihood is that it will be converted for agricultural use. Although the consequences of killing an elephant can result is five years in prison and a fine of 100 million rupiah (about US$10,000), the Sumatran Elephant's time is running out and the clock is ticking.

Red Wolf

Canis rufus

KEY FACTS

» Became extinct in the wild in 1980 due to a combination of aggressive predator control, loss of habitat and widespread hybridisation with Coyotes.

» Captive breeding has enabled a wild population to be re-established, but with just 45–60 wild individuals as of 2016 it is still considered to be the rarest wolf in the world.

» Dispersal of packs due to habitat fragmentation leads to hybridisation with Coyotes.

» Coyotes have been sterilised to stop them breeding with Red Wolves.

» Gunshot wounds have caused a 50 per cent decrease in the reintroduced wild Red Wolf population since 2012.

» Wild Red Wolves can live for 6–7 years, while in captivity this increases to 15 years.

» Red Wolves pair for life. Inbreeding with first-degree relatives is rare.

The rarest wolf

The Red Wolf, *Canis rufus* or known by some as *Canis lupus rufus*, is also called the Florida Wolf or the Mississippi Valley Wolf, reflecting its distribution in the south-eastern USA. The IUCN has listed it as Critically Endangered since 1996 and it is protected under US law. It is thought to be the rarest wolf in the world.

The Red Wolf is between a Timber Wolf and a Coyote in size, with an adult measuring 136–160cm (53.5–63in) and weighing between 23–39kg (50–85lb). Its fur is ashy-black with a reddish cast. It has paler markings around the muzzle and eyes, with a blackish bushy tail. The shoulder height is 38–40cm (15–16in) and at first glance it resembles a German Shepherd dog with long agile limbs. It has particularly big ears.

Species or hybrid?

The taxonomy of the Red Wolf has been greatly contested, especially since 1973 when captive breeding began. Results of a study in October 2012 indicated that the Red Wolf, Timber Wolf and Coyote all diverged from common ancestors 150,000–300,000 years ago. Genetic studies in 2011 and 2016 indicated that the Red Wolf is a hybrid between the Timber Wolf and Coyote, although other studies have suggested that it is an independent species but that hybridisation has occurred with Coyotes due to the fragmentation of Red Wolf packs. It has been shown that where there are packs of similar species within reach, the Red Wolf and the Timber Wolf are less likely to interbreed with Coyotes.

The IUCN takes the view that the Red Wolf is a unique species and has listed it as Critically Endangered since 1996. By 1999, the integration of the Coyote gene was seen to be the most damaging threat to the continued existence of the Red Wolf. Sterilisation of Coyotes has been successful, reducing the Coyote gene to less than 4 per cent of the Red Wolf population by 2015.

Communication and family structure

The Red Wolf is known to be crepuscular, which means they are most dynamic at dawn or dusk. However, they can also be nocturnal. They communicate through a variety of means, including scent-marking, vocalisations (howling and a series of barks, yaps and growling), body language and facial expressions. Its howl is similar to that of a Coyote but lasts longer and is lower pitched. The wolf is shy and secretive, hunting alone or in small packs. Red Wolf packs are smaller than those of the Timber Wolf.

Red Wolf pair bonds last for life and their pack structure will be made up of the alpha male and female – the breeding pair – and a hierarchy of dominant and subordinate wolves, made up of their offspring from a variety of litters. They form a very close-knit unit. The role of older offspring is to attend the den and help with looking after the younger wolves.

Dens are made in hollow trees, stream banks and sandy knolls. Between 1–3 years of age the offspring will go in search of their own domain and partner. Each pack has its own home range, which is their hunting ground, leading them to defend it from other canids. They are very territorial, fighting off other wolves if necessary. They mark their home range heavily with scent as a warning to other packs.

BREEDING

The Red Wolf is a more sociable animal than the Coyote which usually travel in small packs of 2–3, but less so than the Timber Wolf, which hunt in packs of 3–30. They tend to be very shy and secretive. The mating season runs from January to March with a gestation period of 60–63 days, leading to the pups being born in April or May. There can be 3–12 pups in a litter, but the average number is 6–7. Their eyes open at 10 days.

Both parents help to look after the young, including hunting and returning with food. All members of the pack will keep a close eye on the pups, making sure that they do not stray. They will move the den to different locations for the first few months as the scent will become too strong and it will attract the attention of other wolf packs who could eat the young pups. The pups will reach adult size within a year, but they are not considered mature until they are 22–24 months old. They reach sexual maturity at three years.

Inbreeding within the group and with first-degree relatives can result in reduced fitness for the offspring, and thankfully is a rare event. The common pattern is a union between two unrelated wolves, who go on to form a new home range. Avoidance of inbreeding strategies include pups dispersing widely from their pack, either as lone wolves or in a small, non-breeding pack made up of unrelated animals.

EXTINCTION IN THE WILD AND CAPTIVE BREEDING

Originally the range of the Red Wolf extended throughout the eastern United States, from the Atlantic coast to central Texas, and from northern Pennsylvania and the Ohio River Valley to the Gulf of Mexico. It suffered badly in the mid-20th century from aggressive predator control, loss of habitat and widespread hybridisation with Coyotes.

The US Fish and Wildlife Service began serious attempts at saving the Red Wolf in 1973, starting a captive-breeding scheme at Point Defiance in Washington State. They captured 400 wolves in Louisiana and Texas between 1973 and 1980. Efforts were made to distinguish Red Wolves from Coyotes and Red Wolf-Coyote hybrids. Just 43 of the 400 captured animals were thought to be Red Wolves, and with further work this was whittled down to 17 pure-bred Red Wolves. Three of these were unable to breed, which left 14 animals, but since they were so genetically similar they had the effect of only being eight individuals.

These 14 Red Wolves became the basis for captive breeding, with the first litter produced in May 1977. The Red Wolf became extinct in the wild in 1980.

REINTRODUCTION TO THE WILD

The Point Defiance project released 63 Red Wolves into the wild between 1987–1994, and by 2012 the population was estimated to be 100–120 animals in the wild, although unfortunately that number had decreased to 50–75 by 2015. There are around 155 wolves in captivity with 37 captive-breeding projects in operation in the USA. In captivity, a Red Wolf can live to 15 years of age, but this is reduced to an average of 6–7 years in the wild.

Red Wolves have been reintroduced to the wild in north-eastern North Carolina, where they inhabit a territory of 6,850km² (2,645 miles²). This includes 4,050km² (1,565 miles²) of privately owned land and 2,800 km² (1,080 miles²) of state and federal land.

A large number of wolves were found to be suffering from heart worm – a disease which can put human life in jeopardy. They have been medicated and are under observation. Other situations have been of concern too. In 1989 a population of wolves was released on Horn Island in the Mississippi Coast. The wolves in this project suffered from environmental disease and from competition with Coyotes. There was also a problem with low prey density, so in 1998 these animals were relocated to the North Carolina project.

Habitat mysteries

Little is known about the preferred habitat of the Red Wolf. Looking at their historical distribution, which covers a wide range of habitats from south-eastern Texas to central Pennsylvania, it is likely that Red Wolves are generalists and can thrive in most settings where they are supported by adequate prey and do not suffer too much persecution by humans.

The last wild Red Wolf packs were found using coastal prairie marshes, swamps and agricultural fields that grew rice and cotton. Historically, evidence shows that they would have lived in the once extensive bottomland forests and swamps in the south-eastern USA. The wolves reintroduced in North Carolina utilise a range of habitats including wetlands, forests and agricultural land.

Preventing a second extinction

Threats to the reintroduced animals include habitat fragmentation and disease, but perhaps the two greatest hazards are hybridisation with Coyotes, which endangers the Red Wolf's long-term viability as a unique species, and persecution by humans.

More than 150 animals have been released so far during the North Carolina reintroduction. In 2014 the US Fish and Wildlife Service issued the first permit to kill a wolf to a private landowner. Subsequently the USFWS has issued several other permits to landowners in the designated reintroduction range. In June 2015, a landowner shot and killed a female Red Wolf, leading to a public outcry. A lawsuit was filed by the Southern Environmental Law Centre against USFWS for violating the Endangered Species Act.

The 2016 estimate of the Red Wolf population in North Carolina was 45–60 animals, down from 100–120 in 2012. Illegal killing of wolves by humans is a big problem, and death from gunshot wounds is the most significant cause of the decline. In response, the National Wildlife Federation has offered a large reward for information on hunters.

African Wild Dog

Lycaon pictus

KEY FACTS

» The species was highly regarded by predynastic Egyptians and features in cave paintings by the San people of southern Africa.

» The dogs have exceptionally long large intestines and stomachs, allowing them to absorb more water and therefore last longer without a drink.

» More than 80 per cent of wild dog hunts end in a kill – by comparison lions have a success rate of 10 per cent.

» African Wild Dogs formerly occurred in 42 African countries.

» Today less than 5,000 animals remain in the deserts and savannahs of Sub-Saharan Africa.

» Packs may be as large as 40 animals. A group of less than six cannot hunt efficiently.

» As habitats become fragmented, it is harder for the dogs to access other packs to breed. Pack size therefore decreases, making them no longer viable, and that is a key reason that the species is very close to extinction.

WILD DOG HISTORY

The African Wild Dog has many names, including African Hunting Dog, African Painted Dog or, as the scientific name translates, Painted Wolf. It used to be found in 42 African counties but now occurs only sporadically in the deserts, open plains and arid savannahs of Sub-Saharan Africa. Current figures estimate that there are 38 populations made up of 5,000 dogs. The main threats to the wild dog are habitat fragmentation, hunting by humans and disease.

Historically, the species was highly regarded by the predynastic Egyptians, where depictions of the animal feature on cosmetic palettes and other objects. The San people give it a mystical role, seeing the dog as the ultimate hunter and believing that their shamans can transform into the dog, giving them special powers. There are very few fossil finds of the dog, so its evolution is not well known.

Coat of many shades

The African Wild Dog exhibits bright mottled fur with patches of red, orange, brown, black and white, which helps to break up its outline and hide it from potential prey and predators. It is also an aid to identification as no two dogs are the same, and their coat pattern is as unique as a human fingerprint. Since they have incredibly good eyesight it is thought that they they can recognise each other from distances of up to 100m (330ft). The dog's fur is stiff and bristle-like with no underfur, and animals experience hair-loss with age. A white plume on the tip of the tail is thought to help members of a pack to keep in contact while hunting, when it is raised high and acts like a flag.

This dog is the bulkiest canid in Africa. It stands 65–75cm (26–30in) at the shoulder and weighs up to 36kg (80lb). They measure 1.5m (5ft) from head to tail, with a tail length of 30–40cm (12–16in). Females are 4–8 per cent smaller than males.

They lack dewclaws and their middle two toepads are combined, giving them four toes instead of the normal five. They have exceptionally large intestines and stomach, allowing them to absorb more water from their food so that they can last for longer periods without needing a drink. They are quite long-legged and have large bat-like ears. Their molar and premolar teeth are larger than those found in other canids, allowing them to crush bones easily. Their life expectancy is 10–13 years.

Pack dynamics

The wild dog's home range is large; around 1000km² (620mi²) depending on the size of the prey population. When a litter is born, activity becomes closer to the den. There are often more males in a pack than females and they both form their own hierarchy. The dominant pair will be the only breeding pair, and they are made up of the oldest female and the oldest male, unless he is superseded by a younger male. Packs can be as large as 40 dogs, but are often 10–30 strong. Most pack members will be interrelated. A pack of less than six will not be able to hunt efficiently. They are very sociable creatures and will do everything together including hunting, sharing food, raising young and looking after sick dogs. Unusually, it is the females that leave the natal pack rather than the males. They will join other packs and evict females that they find there, thus curbing interbreeding.

The hierarchy is based on submission rather than dominance. The reason being that hunting efficiency must be maintained and a wounded dog would be of no use to the pack. A dog will beg to gain food rather than resort to conflict.

COMMUNICATION

One way the African Wild Dog communicates is by vocalisation. They have a series of calls including a rallying howl, a bark of alarm, and a bell-like call that can be heard for miles around. They prepare for hunting by moving round other pack members, making high-pitched barks and nosing and licking one another until excitement increases and they are ready for the hunt.

They hunt co-operatively, with some dogs chasing close to the prey and others waiting in the wings a little further behind, ready to take the lead when the first dogs tire. The dogs' stamina and perseverance makes them highly successful hunters, with 80 per cent of their chases ending in a kill. As a comparison the success rate for lion hunts is just 10 per cent.

African Wild Dogs have few natural predators, although lions and hyenas have been known to prey on them in very rare cases when an individual becomes isolated.

BIG LITTERS

There is no fixed breeding season for wild dogs in eastern Africa, although in southern Africa they breed in the late rainy season, between March and June. After a gestation period of 68–73 days they produce a litter of 6–19 pups, which is the largest of any canid – enough to form a new pack every year. The mother waits 12 months before becoming pregnant again, allowing her first litter to mature. However, few pups live to see adulthood, due to factors such as dens becoming flooded, and loss to predators, disease or exposure.

The pups are important to the pack as they ensure its continued welfare and existence. All members of the pack are involved in their care, including babysitting and providing food. Occasionally, a submissive female will be allowed to breed with another male, but the dominant female has been known to kill her pups.

The pups are born in a den made from thick bush or grass, or in another animal's abandoned den. The mother will suckle the pups in the den until they are 3–4 weeks old, driving other pack members away. She will then take them outside to be suckled. They are weaned at five weeks, from which point they are fed regurgitated food by other pack members. At 8–10 weeks old the mother will abandon the den and the pups will follow the adults in the hunt. The pups are allowed to feed on the kill first, until they are yearlings when they must wait their turn. They can fend for themselves when they are 14 months old and are sexually mature at 12–18 months.

It is rare to find inbreeding in a pack, Habitats are becoming more fragmented, which is a cause for concern, making it harder for animals to move from one pack to other in order to introduce fresh genes.

HUNTING WITH STAMINA

The pack approaches its prey in full view. Surprise is not an advantage as the dogs use their stamina to chase prey to exhaustion. Although the prey may be faster, the endurance of the dogs will win the day more often than not. The dogs can maintain speeds of 60kph (37mph) for up to 60 minutes. The prey can zigzag, which can confuse lone hunters such as cheetahs, but the dog pack counters this by spreading out to prevent escape.

The dogs will call to each other with high-pitched yaps, and as the prey slows down from exhaustion they start to rip at its underbelly. Like other predators, wild dogs play a role in maintaining a healthy ecosystem by culling weak and old animals from the populations of prey species. An average of three kills per day are needed in order to sustain the pack. Wild dogs are not scavengers and they will not revisit an earlier kill.

Wild dogs rely upon the sense of sight rather than smell in order to co-ordinate the hunt. They live mostly in savannahs, arid zones and open woodlands, usually avoiding forest, which allows them to see greater distances. However, they will travel through woodland, upland areas and scrub while pursuing prey. The most common prey items are medium-sized ungulates including zebra and antelopes such as gazelles, impalas and springboks. They will occasionally hunt large birds such as ostriches. Wildebeest can weigh 250kg (550lb), but they will be considered prey if they have become isolated due to illness or if the wild dog pack is big enough. Smaller prey items include spring hares, cane rats and dik-diks.

THREATS FROM LIONS AND HYENAS

Wild dogs are in competition with lions and hyenas as they all hunt the same prey.

Lions are a threat to wild dogs, and in areas where lions are prevalent the dogs will be scarce. One pack of wild dogs that was reintroduced to Etosha National Park, Namibia, was decimated by lions. If the lion population decreases for any reason, then there is a good chance that the wild dog population will take an upward turn.

Spotted Hyenas will follow wild dog packs in order to feed. Groups of hyenas can hijack a dog kill, although the dogs' ability to work as a pack gives them the advantage against a lone hyena in protecting their kill. However, overall if there is a high density of hyenas in an area there tends to be a low density of African Wild Dogs.

POPULATIONS IN AFRICA TODAY

Today the African Wild Dog lives in southern Africa and southern parts of east Africa, with Tanzania and Mozambique hosting good sized populations. Throughout Africa, wild dogs have been persecuted by farmers, who view them as a threat to cattle and other livestock and shoot or poison them, as well as rangers and hunters, who dislike their habit of scattering of wild animal herds.

The wild dog is a very rare sight indeed nowadays. They often live in national parks, but frequently a pack's home range is greater than the area of land protected by the park, bringing even these animals into conflict with humans. As wild dog populations decrease, so does pack size, making them no longer viable and bringing them closer to extinction. With less than 5,000 individuals left in Africa, the threats of hunting, habitat fragmentation and disease caught from livestock make the species' future survival prospects appear somewhat precarious.

South China Tiger

Panthera tigris amoyensis

KEY FACTS

» Thought to be extinct in the wild.

» In May 2007, the Chinese Government declared that it would reintroduce the South China Tiger back into its natural habitat.

» A crucial component to this project's success is the rehabilitation of prey populations. They need large numbers of prey species such as deer, antelope and boar in their territory in order to thrive. The complete food chain and its associated biodiversity must therefore be restored.

» The rewilding process involves giving captive tigers months of training in learning how to hunt.

» While a female is nurturing her cubs, she will not breed again, but a male who is looking to mate with her will kill her existing cubs.

» The South China Tigers are showing a lot of Indochinese Tiger genes, which, in the opinion of experts, puts doubt over the logic of saving them.

HISTORIC RANGE

The South China Tiger, also known as the Chinese Tiger, Amoy Tiger or Xiamen Tiger, originally inhabited a range encompassing 2,000km (1,250 miles) from west to east and 1,500km (930 miles) from north to south, taking in the Chinese provinces of Fujian, Hunan, Guizhou, Guangdong and Jiangxi. Its habitat varied from evergreen forests to rocky mountains, damp tropical forests and coastal areas. South China Tigers have a pronounced morphology and the current thinking is that they could be the forebearer of all tigers.

A PALE ORANGE TIGER

Adult males measure 2.3–2.7m (7.5–8.7ft) and weigh in the region of 150–177kg (330–390lb). Females are slightly smaller at 2.0–2.4m (6–7.9ft), weighing about 123kg (270lb). Compared to other tigers, South China Tigers have a smaller cranial region, with their eyes positioned closer together, and shorter molars. They have a paler, more yellow-orange coat with fewer, thinner stripes. They are also whiter on the paws, face, inside leg and stomach. Their fur length varies according to climate and they can live in different temperature zones.

In the wild they typically choose to inhabit upland forest, hunting after sunset and living solitarily unless breeding or looking after cubs. The range of each animal is in the region of 70km² (27 mi²) and in this area they need roughly 200 Spotted Deer, 350 antelopes and 150 Wild Boars to support them. They will eat 18–45kg (40–100lb) of meat in one go, and then not eat for several days. Smaller prey such as porcupines or rabbits will be taken if no other food is available. They hunt prey down and attack from the side, aiming for the throat. Once downed, they drag their quarry for up to a few hundred metres until they reach an area where they can conceal the kill and will start to eat. They are top of their food chain, with their only danger being humans. They can swim but are unable to climb trees.

BREEDING HABITS

The breeding season runs from the end of November until the middle of April. Female South China Tigers are sexually mature at four years of age, while males are ready to breed at five years. When ready to mate, a female emits a distinct smell which she leaves traces of around her home range.

The gestation period is 103 days, and 3–6 cubs are born in a litter. The female will build a shelter in which to give birth as the babies are born blind and relatively small at 780–1,600g (1.7–3.5lb). They suckle from their mother for eight weeks and she will continue hunting during this period in order to produce milk for them, needing to eat 150 per cent more than usual to do this.

The mortality rate for the young is 50 per cent in the first two years. The female will teach them to hunt by the time they are six months old and they will be independent by the age of 1.5–2 years. While a female is nurturing her cubs she will not breed again, but a male who is looking to mate with her will kill her existing cubs. In the wild, a tiger can expect to live to about 15 years, while in captivity this is increased to about 20 years thanks to the benefits of healthcare, readily available food and protection.

DIMINISHING TO THE POINT OF EXTINCTION IN THE WILD

South China Tigers have faced the dangers of habitat loss, and subsequent loss of prey over the years. The wide-reaching 'anti-pest' offensive of Mao Zedong's 'Great Leap Forward' in the late 1950s and early 1960s saw unlimited hunting and widespread deforestation that effectively reduced the tiger population from 4,000 individuals to 150–200 tigers by 1982. The trend was spiralling so that by 1987 population estimates were in the region of just 30–40 animals. Eleven reserves were searched in 1990 and signs of the tigers were found, but no tigers were spotted. The only evidence were signs of tracks and sightings by local people. By 2001, GPS technology and camera traps were installed in eight protected regions covering 2,214km² (855mi²). No tigers were seen.

Government Protection

The Chinese government was slow to act regarding the impending extinction of the South China Tiger. In 1973 it authorised the controlled hunting of tigers, but by 1977 hunting was prohibited and the tigers became protected. Both national and international trade in tigers was banned in 2007.

In May 2007, the Chinese Government announced the absence of the South China Tiger in the wild and declared that it would be reintroduced back into its natural habitat. The intention is to sustain three populations of 15–20 tigers, with a minimum range of 1,000km² (386 miles²) per group. A crucial component to this project's success is the rehabilitation of prey populations.

Genetic Diversity of Captive Tigers

Among the captive tigers available to the Chinese Government there are problems with inbreeding and therefore a lack of genetic variance. The problems lie with the starter stock, which was made up of one female from Fujian and five males from Guizhou captured from the wild in 1956. There are also issues with low breeding productivity. However, by March 1986, 40 pedigree South China Tigers had been born in captivity; 23 of these were male and 17 female. They were all third or fourth generation tigers from the starting stock. Male captive tigers have a reduced sperm count and little inclination to mate. Cubs are born with birth imperfections and increased mortality rates. Cancers originating from pollution and food additives are responsible for 50 per cent of deaths in mature tigers. China aims to expand genetic diversity by using a centrally registered stud book.

Sites for Rewilding

The year 2001 saw the start of South Africa's involvement in the project, working together with the Chinese State Forestry Administration. They were able to find nine sites in China that passed the 36 ecological parameters set, with the aim of rewilding the tiger. Rewilding is a term started by Gus Van

Dyke in 2003, which outlines the process of teaching captive tigers to hunt again with a view to releasing them into the wild. The contract to rewild South China Tigers was signed in Beijing on 26 November 2002. This rewilding process takes place in South Africa, on a private reserve in the Laohu Valley.

REWILDING CATHAY AND HOPE

In September 2003, two cubs named Cathay and Hope were sent from Shanghai Zoo to Laohu for training. They did not respond well to attempts to get them hunting. Initially they were shown a chicken, which stared them down and frightened them. The team's next step was to put some chicken meat into the cub's food and then throw a plucked chicken into their cage. They followed that up by introducing a dead chicken with its feathers intact, and the cubs finally began to get a grip on what they were supposed to do.

REWILDING TIGER WOODS AND MADONNA

Two more cubs – a male named Tiger Woods and a female called Madonna – were introduced to Laohu Valley in late 2004. They had also been born at Shanghai Zoo. It took them months to make the link between food and a kill. At first, they were too timid to even leave their cage. They spent a month at a 0.4ha (1 acre) quarantine camp, moving on to a 4ha (10 acre) area for three months. During that time they were able to bring down their first antelope. Seeing that their natural instincts had been ignited, the team transferred them to a 60ha (150 acre) enclosure where they learned to refine their skills. From there, they were moved to a 6,000 ha (14,800 acre) area that was fenced. With the addition of radio collars the team could monitor their hunting skills and follow their activity until they were considered to have been successfully rewilded.

RE-ESTABLISHING BIODIVERSITY THROUGH REWILDING

Laohu Valley Reserve started off as a region of 17 overgrazed sheep farms in very bad condition and with no evidence of any healthy ecosystem. It is now one of the largest protected areas in South Africa. It works by taking the starting point that tigers are an apex predator carnivore, and by protecting this species and its prey the complete food chain and the attached biodiversity is also restored. In other words, through supporting the tiger, its habitat also gets rehabilitated. Laohu has become a recognised leader in re-establishing South African biodiversity. China has taken note, and conservationists there are aiming to restore tiger habitat in Jiangxi and Hunan provinces. Recreating the forest environment could be a lengthy process as the area is currently farmland.

PROBLEMS FACING REWILDING IN CHINA

Two other obstacles stand in the way of success. One is the cost of the project, which is set at 180 million yuan (approximately US$2.5million). This includes the cost of relocating quite a few human settlements.

There is also the question of genetic makeup. The South China Tigers are showing a lot of Indochinese Tiger genes, which, in the opinion of the experts, casts doubt over the logic of saving them.

Sumatran Tiger

Panthera tigris sumatrae

KEY FACTS

» A rare subspecies of tiger found only on the Indonesian island of Sumatra.

» Between 441–679 are thought to remain in the wild, living in isolated pockets of habitat.

» A further 100 Sumatran Tigers can be found in zoos and safari parks.

» The logging industry has had a huge impact on tiger habitat in Sumatra, with the area of land used by the palm oil industry increasing fivefold in the last 10 years, with more to follow.

» There is still a massive market in Asia for tiger commodities, with bones fetching the highest price. This trade is responsible for 78 per cent of tiger mortalities annually.

» Indonesian law gives heavy fines and jail sentences for the killing of a tiger.

LAST OF THE ISLAND TIGERS

A scarce subspecies of tiger found only on the Indonesian island of Sumatra. It is part of the Sunda Island group of tigers, which also contained the Bali Tiger and the Javan Tiger, but both of these are now extinct, leaving the Sumatran Tiger as the only living member of the group.

There are thought to be between 441–679 Sumatran Tigers remaining in the wild, living in isolated pockets of forest in populations of no more than 50 animals. Evidence suggests that this small population is still in decline.

CHARACTERISTICS

The Sumatran Tiger has an orange coat with thick black stripes that are bigger than those of the Javan Tiger and set closer together than in other tigers. The stripes often split and have paler markings in the middle, forming lines on the back, flanks and hind legs. The tigers' habitat contains long grass and their heavy striping aids them in terms of providing camouflage.

The males have a characteristic beard and mane which also covers their cheeks and neck. Available prey is significantly smaller than prey that other tigers consume, so the Sumatran Tiger is slighter than most other tiger subspecies. Males are 2.2–2.55m (7.2–8.4ft) long and weigh 100–140kg (220–310lb). Females are smaller, measuring 2.15–2.3m (7.1–7.5ft) long and weighing 75–110kg (165–243lb). Even though the Sumatran Tiger is much less weighty than say the Bengal Tiger, it is still able to rupture the legs of horses and buffalos with its mighty paws.

PREHISTORIC ROOTS AND DNA

The Sumatran Tiger split from other tiger populations during the Pleistocene and Holocene border, 12,000 to 6,000 years ago. DNA analysis shows that it is genetically distinct from extant mainland tigers. However, this does not work in its favour. The tigers that are left in Sumatra are very closely related with very similar genes. DNA testing of tigers for captive breeding selects genetically separate individuals before allowing them to mate. If their DNA was too similar the resulting cubs would suffer birth defects and have a higher risk of mortality while young.

BREEDING

The tigers mate between November and April. The female gives off a powerful scent to alert males in the proximity. The breeding pair will call to each other in the forest in order to detect one another. Once they have met, they will mate several times over a three- or four-day interval.

The female makes a shelter and gives birth to up to six cubs, although two or three is the most common size for a litter. They remain in the safety of the shelter for eight weeks, with the mother going off to hunt occasionally so that she can produce milk to feed them.

WHAT'S ON THE MENU?

The prey of these tigers includes Malay Tapir, wild pig, porcupine, Great Argus pheasant, pig-tailed macaque and deer such as Greater and Lesser Mouse-Deer, Sambar and Muntjac. Tigers are at the top of the food chain in Sumatra. A decrease in tiger numbers accelerates the growth of populations of their prey species, undermining the natural balance of the ecosystem.

HUMAN-TIGER CONFLICT

The palm oil industry has increased fivefold in the last 10 years, and the Indonesian government is keen to increase its share further. As land is lost, there is a marked reduction in the tiger's habitat and prey base. Palm oil, together with the logging industry, have had a huge effect on tiger territory, especially in lowland forest, precipitating a sharp decrease in tiger numbers. Agricultural development is continuing even within Tesso Nilo National Park boundaries. Tigers are relocated to the centre of the park in an effort to save them.

Human-tiger clashes are a source of tension in Sumatra. Tigers are forced into areas of human settlement because they are hungry. Habitat destruction has reduced the availability of their prey species and they turn to agricultural settlements in their search for food. They have become more aggressive as their habitat decreases as they are driven into competition with other tigers in their fight for survival. Farmers will kill a tiger in order to protect themselves. One tiger produces 10 years' income on the black market.

LAW AND THE BLACK MARKET

There is still a massive market in Asia for tiger commodities. These include skin, bones, canines and whiskers; with bones fetching the highest prices with canines coming in second. One tiger produces the equivalent of 10 years' income on the black market. This market is responsible for 78 per cent of tiger mortalities annually, and there is no indication that it will change in the near future.

Indonesian law gives heavy fines and jail sentences for the killing of a tiger. The government has made a real effort to protect the tiger. Laws have been toughened and antipoaching work has been increased.

LAST HABITAT

Tigers thrive in wide variety of habitats, ranging from lowland forests by the sea to elevations of 3,200m (10,500ft) above sea-level. They select uncultivated forest, staying deep in its centre and normally avoiding all contact with human settlement and agriculture. They require a cover of dense understory in order to hunt. Their range is large, and surveys in Tesso Nilo National Park in 2005 reported a tiger density of 0.90 tigers per 100km² (39 miles²). Unfortunately, presumably due to habitat loss, this figure is on the increase, and by 2008 the density of tigers was reported to be 1.70 per 100km² (39 miles²).

It is a serious situation. Sumatra is unique in that it is the only location left on Earth where elephants, tigers, rhinos and orangutans are found in unison surviving in the wild. That makes the island a very special place, rich in biodiversity. The loss of the tiger would significantly alter that.

Illegal Clearance

There has been a total loss of jurisdiction in some parts of the island of Sumatra. Around 67,178km² (25,938miles²) of forest, which is an area comparable in size to Scotland, were cleared between 1986 and 1997 due to illegal logging and conversion to agriculture.

The Indonesian government has turned a corner, and more recently has been working hard to conserve the tiger's habitat. In 2009, the president made a pledge to significantly minimise deforestation. Since then the equivalent to US$210 million has been spent on reinforcing the law regarding tigers, concentrating mainly on anti-poaching. There is little evidence to show that this has been successful.

Environmental Margarine

In 2010 a profit-making business initiative for tiger preservation proved very successful. The product was 'tiger friendly' margarine, made using vegetables rather than palm oil. Research surmised that people were happy to pay more for a good class product that would help the environmental cause.

Tigers in captivity

There are in the region of 100 Sumatran Tigers living in zoos and safari parks. The only sperm bank is at the captive-breeding centre at Taman Safari in West Java, Indonesia.

Sumatran Tigers are being born in captivity. The 44,515ha (110,000 acre) preservation and rehabilitation reserve of Tambling Wildlife Nature Conservation in Lampung, Sumatra, had a surprise birth in October 2011. A young female which had been captured earlier that month with a wounded leg successfully gave birth to four male cubs.

Other births in captivity include three cubs born to a five-year-old female in February 2014 in the prestigious Tiger Territory in London Zoo, UK. This establishment cost US$5 million to erect and is specifically designed to support the captive-breeding of rare tigers, and there was further success with two more cubs produced in June 2016.

Mountain Gorilla

Gorilla beringei beringei

KEY FACTS

» Today just two populations remain – one in Bwindi Forest in Uganda and the other in the Virunga Mountains bordering Rwanda, Uganda and the Democratic Republic of Congo.

» The total population numbered 880 in September 2012. Numbers reached an all-time low of only 254 individuals in 1981.

» The gorilla's home range is decided by food availability, spanning a wide range of altitudes with foods such as wild celery, nettles, thistles and bracket fungi making up crucial components of its diet.

» More than 20 per cent of gorilla deaths (especially respiratory deaths) are caused by human cross-infection, and measles, flu, scabies, salmonella and Ebola have all been passed from humans to gorillas.

» Political instability in the region containing gorilla habitat is putting 20 years of valuable conservation practice at risk.

» In its lifetime each gorilla can generate US$3.5 million in income through ecotourism. For example, more than 20,000 visitors to Uganda in 2008 raised around US$8 million for conservation.

Mountain Gorilla populations

Fossil finds show the existence of ape-like primates in East Africa 22–32 million years ago. It is thought that gorillas evolved as separate species approximately 9 million years ago.

Today there are two distinct populations of Mountain Gorilla remaining, with one in the Bwindi Impenetrable National Park, Uganda, and the other in the Virunga Mountains, a volcanic range with peaks up to 4,300m (14,100ft) spanning the borders of Rwanda, Uganda and the Democratic Republic of Congo (DRC). The IUCN classified these two populations as representing two different subspecies in 2003. The two populations combined numbered 880 in September 2012, and the species is listed as Critically Endangered.

Habitat and sexual dimorphism

Mountain Gorillas have denser fur than other gorillas since the temperature in their habitat often drops below freezing. They have a unique nose print, similar to the unique finger prints of humans.

The species exhibits marked sexual dimorphism, with males weighing an average of 195kg (439lb) and being approximately double the weight of females, which average 100kg (220lb). When standing males measure 1.5m (4.9ft), whereas females are 1.3m (4.3ft). They are second only to the Eastern Lowland Gorilla in terms of height.

Males have a distinct bony crest at the top and back of their skull, exhibiting a profuse crest of fur. This allows the muscles that attach to the bottom jaw to be extremely powerful. Females lack this strength. An adult male is known as a 'silverback' due to the silvery hair that develops on the back with age. These gorillas live for 40–50 years in the wild, and moderately longer in zoos.

Walking on all fours

Mountain Gorillas have longer arms than legs, so they usually walk on all fours, holding their hands in a fist and using their knuckles to take their enormous bulk. The Common Chimpanzee uses the same method. The gorilla can climb up a tree as long as the branches will support its great weight, while they can run on two legs for distances of up to 10m (33ft).

REST AND NEST

A Mountain Gorilla likes to sleep throughout the night, and is most active between sunrise and sunset, which is approximately from 6am to 6pm. They will generally scavenge until midday, which is when the sun is hottest, and then rest during the afternoon. They need to eat a great deal in order to maintain energy levels in their enormous body. They will create a nest every evening using available vegetation such as branches and grasses. Each adult has a separate nest, but infants sleep with their mother.

A MOSTLY VEGETARIAN DIET

The Mountain Gorilla's diet is 99 per cent herbivorous, with 86 per cent coming from the leaves, stems and shoots of the 142 plant species available in their habitat. Tree bark accounts for 6 per cent of the remainder, while 3 per cent is from roots, 2 per cent from flowers, 2 per cent from fruit, and the balancing 1 per cent is made up of protein from invertebrates such as ants and worms. An adult male will need 34kg (75lb) of food to sustain him each day, while an adult female will need 18kg (40lb).

The gorillas' home range is defined by food availability, and spans different altitudinal biomes. Important feeding grounds include the bamboo forests at 2,200–2,800m (7,200–9,200ft), *Hagenia* forests at 2,800–3,400m (9,200–11,200ft), and the giant *Senecio* zone at 3,400–4,300m (11,200–14,200ft) above sea-level. Food such as wild celery, stinging nettles, thistles, bedstraw and bracket fungi make up a crucial component of their diet, and they derive water from the plants that they eat. With their wide-ranging grazing, gorillas help to maintain the health of the ecosystem to the advantage of all life, including humans, who need the habitat for water-supply, food and other benefits.

MAKE-UP OF GORILLA SOCIETY

Mountain Gorilla groups vary in size from 5–30 individuals, but typically number about 10. They are made up of a dominant silverback who will be in a long-term alliance with several females. A number of infants and juveniles will accompany the females. There may be a subordinate silverback and one or two blackbacks; young males, whose role is to keep guard over the group.

A silverback will be a minimum of 12–15 years old, which is the age of sexual maturity, and will lead the group for an average of 4.7 years. Young males leave the group at around 11 years of age. They will either become solitary or connect with an all-male group which they will leave only when they become sexually active and able to attract a female and begin a new group.

BIRTH AND THE YOUNG

Females can give birth from the age of about 10 and will have a baby every 3–4 years. The gestation period is 8.5 months and babies weigh approximately 1.8kg (4lb) at birth. To begin with they are totally dependent upon their mother and will cling to her for the first 3–4 months, after which they are able to sit and stand, but only with assistance. It takes 3.5 years for them to be weaned and switch to an adult diet. A mother's instinct is to fight to the death if one of her young is threatened.

DOMINANT BEHAVIOUR FROM SILVERBACKS

The silverback looks after the community, defending his family and keeping peace within the group, while also determining times for feeding trips, travel and rest. A group is usually peaceful, however if two silverbacks meet there will be exhibitions of menacing behaviour such as gorillas rising to their feet, beating of the chest, throwing vegetation, stamping of feet, and galloping in a mock attack. Occasionally the silverbacks will fight with their teeth; sometimes to the death.

If a human threatens a gorilla, the gorilla will attack and it is important for the human to stand their ground and not to point, stare, or use other intimidating behaviour.

When the dominant silverback dies the group is left in disarray. Another contender usually kills the young of the previous silverback, leaving only the females, who he will mate with.

INBREEDING AND CROSS-INFECTION FROM HUMANS

Insufficient Mountain Gorilla population sizes have resulted in inbreeding. Subsequently the absence of genetic diversity makes them vulnerable to disease. Contaminated water supplies have resulted in the transmission of hepatitis A and B to Mountain Gorillas, while cross-contamination with water affected by livestock can cause gastro-intestinal problems.

Gorillas are susceptible to human diseases, having comparable DNA, but they lack the progressive immunity. Humans can infect a gorilla with many diseases, including pneumonia, which is a particular danger during cold, wet periods. Measles, flu, scabies, salmonella and Ebola have all been passed from human to gorilla. Studies show that 20 per cent of gorilla deaths, especially respiratory deaths, are caused by human cross-infection. Nowadays, for humans visiting the gorillas, the rule is to stand 7m (20ft) away from the animals in order to reduce the risk of spreading disease.

PREDATORS, PET TRADE AND POPULATION

Predators include other gorillas, crocodiles and leopards. Humans pose the greatest risks for these animals due to factors such as hunting for bushmeat, revenge for crop-raiding, and getting stuck in snares left for antelopes. The black market trade in gorilla heads and hands is a big problem as is the pet trade, where infant gorillas are caught and sold to zoos for anywhere between US$1,000–5,000.

Mountain Gorilla numbers reached an all-time low in 1981 when only 254 individuals were recorded. Through a great deal of conservation work that figure increased to 620 in 1989 and 880 in 2012.

POLITICAL INSTABILITY IN THE REGION

A key concern is political instability in the countries bordering the gorilla habitats. Rwanda, DRC and Uganda have all had problems in the last couple of decades, with an estimated 750,000 Rwandan refugees settling in the area and militia hiding in the forest, while 5.4 million people have died in DRC since 1998.

Direct consequences of the troubles include 13 gorillas being shot during the conflicts, while land mines placed along the trails in the Volcanoes National Park, Rwanda, killed two others. Meanwhile 175 Virunga park rangers have lost their lives since 1996 as the militia have occupied this territory. It is very difficult to work in such conditions, and in 2007 ten gorillas were killed by militia in a deliberate attempt to impede conservation activity.

Habitat loss and emergency measures

Habitat loss is also an issue for the Mountain Gorilla, with shifting (slash and burn) agriculture, encroaching pasture and logging making great inroads into the forest. The local people, living in poverty, use Virunga National Park to collect wood, which they use for heating and cooking.

To prevent refugees logging the forest, the WWF and United Nations have provided emergency wood. Conservation work now focuses on the regrowth of habitat and provision of anti-poaching rangers. However, continuing political instability is putting at risk 20 years of valuable conservation practice.

SUCCESSFUL ECOTOURISM

Ecotourism, which generates significant employment and funds for local communities, is seen as the future for the region. Each gorilla in its lifetime can create US$3.5 million in income through ecotourism. Tourism is thriving in Uganda where, for example, more than 20,000 visitors in 2008 raised around US$8 million, paying not only for the upkeep of the park, but also contributing significantly to the country's overall conservation budget.

Eastern Lowland Gorilla

Gorilla beringei graueri

KEY FACTS

» Found only in the Democratic Republic of Congo (DRC), where reports in 2016 suggested a population of 3,800.

» Groups tend to contain 2–20 individuals, usually with one silverback and up to a handful of females and their young.

» War and political unrest in DRC have made life dangerous for the gorillas, and for conservationists aiming to protect them.

» Young gorillas are abducted to sell to zoos or as pets. Taking an infant usually involves killing the mother as well, and sometimes the entire group.

» Fragmentation of habitat means that inbreeding has become prevalent. The translocation of animals to safe new locations for breeding is being planned.

» The gorilla's habitat is rich in minerals. In 2007, cassiterite worth US$45 million, wolframite worth US$4.3 million and coltan (a valuable component of mobile phones) worth US$5.4 million were exported from the forest.

Largest primate

The Eastern Lowland Gorilla is found in the Democratic Republic of Congo (DRC), living in the lowlands and Albertine Rift montane forests in the east of the country, part of the Virunga Mountain range. A 2004 study reported that there were 5,000 individuals left, however a further report in 2016 suggested there were only 3,800.

It is the largest of all primates, bigger than other gorillas with its stockier body, elongated arms and bigger hands, although it has smaller teeth and a smaller muzzle. Males measure 1.70–1.95m (5.8–6.4ft) high when standing and weigh 200–250kg (450–550lb). Females are smaller, measuring 1.60m (5.2ft) and weighing 100–135kg (220–300lb).

Group structure

The Eastern Lowland Gorilla is similar to the Mountain Gorilla in many respects. Group size ranges from 2–20 individuals, typically with a single silverback and up to a handful of females and their young. The silverback works to gain access to available food and to defend the community from jeopardy and predation. The group tends to be stable and will continue as a unit for months, sometimes years.

Gorillas mature at eight years of age, by which time they will begin to start to leave the group. Females will either connect with another group or find a lone silverback as a mate. Males can regroup in all-male communities as they aren't ready to find a mate for another 4–5 years.

A female gorilla will carry her baby for eight and a half months and will breastfeed for about three years. By the age of nine weeks the baby is ready to crawl, and at 35 weeks it is able to walk. A youngster will keep close to its mother for three or four years. Sexual maturity is reached at 8 years for a female and 12 years for a male.

An ape of all altitudes

The Eastern Lowland Gorilla has the largest altitudinal range of all gorillas. It is found in the highlands of Kahuzi-Biega National Park, which encompasses habitats such as dense primary forest, *Cyperus* swamp, peat bog and moderately moist woodland, and is also able to make its home in mountain areas, transitional zones and lowland tropical forests.

GOING BANANAS

These gorillas do not enjoy eating banana fruit, but they are very fond of the pith inside banana plants. It is full of nutrition and quite often the entire tree is demolished in the eating. This understandably raises the hackles of banana farmers, who find that their crops are ruined and will often kill the gorilla and sell it for bushmeat. The Eastern Lowland Gorilla will also eat fruits, leaves, stems, bark and sometimes ants and termites for protein.

WAR IN DRC

The war in DRC, starting in 1996 and reigniting in 1998, has made it very difficult for research to be carried out on these primates, as well as creating havoc for the gorillas. It has been the most murderous war since World War II. A peace deal was signed in December 2002, with formal involvement from Angola, Rwanda, Namibia, Zimbabwe and Uganda. However, fighting still continues in the east of the country, which is where the Eastern Lowland Gorillas are. Throughout this time, military groups and refugees have taken to the forests, killing gorillas for bushmeat. The military have taken all the weapons from the park rangers so that they have no control over what goes on in the forest, while government funding for national parks has ceased. Before the civil war, in the mid-1990s, there were thought to be 17,000 Eastern Lowland Gorillas in the forest. It is estimated that more than 80 per cent of the gorillas in the forest have been killed, although precise records are hard to ascertain.

MINERALS IN THE FOREST

Multinational companies buy forest products in cash, which is used to fund the war. The gorilla's habitat is rich in cassiterite – 14,700 tons, worth US$45 million, were exported in 2007. In the same year 1,200 tons of wolframite, worth US$4.30 million, were also exported, along with 400 tons of coltan with a value of US$5.40 million. Coltan is particularly sought after on the global exchange as it is a valuable component of mobile phones. It is found extensively inside the gorilla's habitat. Control over these mineral rich territories fuels the war.

RWANDAN GENOCIDE

The Rwandan genocide in 1994 bought 2 million refugees into Tanzania and DRC. It is thought that there were up to 750,000 refugees making camp around Virunga National Park in five key areas; Katale, Kahindo, Kibumba, Mugunga and Lac Vert. With the start of the war in DRC in 1996 life became even more dangerous and approximately half a million of these refugees stayed within the park boundaries. The forest is decreasing by about 10ha (25 acres) daily as the refugees log trees from the forest for firewood. The availability of bushmeat in the forest, including that of the Eastern Lowland Gorilla, increases the chances of these refugees staying.

BUSHMEAT AND INFANT ABDUCTION

Studies have gathered evidence that 5 million metric tons of bushmeat are traded per annum. This quantity includes great apes, chimpanzees and bonobos, which make up 0.5–2 per cent of the total. About 300 Eastern Lowland Gorillas are 'harvested' each year. It is catastrophic for the gorilla, which already has incredibly vulnerable communities and a slow rate of reproduction that means it takes a very long time to recover populations.

Infant gorillas are abducted to sell to zoos or as pets. Taking an infant usually involves killing the mother as well, if not the entire group of gorillas, who all try and protect the baby. Gorilla parts are also used in traditional medicine and as magic charms.

GREAT WAR OF AFRICA

By 2008, the Great War of Africa or Second Congo War, as it was known, had claimed 5.4 million lives, mostly due to disease or starvation as international aid agencies were denied access to them. Two million refugees were created. Nine African countries and 25 militia groups were involved. This hostility, which continues to this day, has been over the illegal exploitation of diamonds, cobalt, coltan, gold and further conflict minerals from the Congo by other countries and organisations.

There are initiatives in place in the wider world to prevent the use of conflict minerals. It is very difficult to trace their country of origin, and they frequently go through several agents prior to purchase. Schemes such as the Dodd-Frank Wall Street Protection Act in the US, in 2010, made it compulsory for producers to investigate their supply chains and publicise the employment of conflict minerals.

The atmosphere in Virunga National Park has been incredibly heated. Over the last 20 years, 175 park rangers working across national boundaries have been killed in the line of duty. They have been doing some extremely perilous work by attempting to halt the movement of unlawful forest products.

INBREEDING AND TRANSLOCATION

The fragmentation of habitat is creating consequences in terms of inbreeding, which reduces the gorilla's ability to adapt to its environment. Some experts suggest that the Eastern Lowland Gorilla is actually two subspecies, with insufficient individuals as founders of the communities. This, coupled with a lack of ability to migrate far, has meant that inbreeding has become the norm. Experts say that translocating particular gorillas to specified locations and starting a captive-breeding initiative will be two important steps towards preserving the species.

Bornean Orangutan

Pongo pygmaeus

KEY FACTS

» The largest tree-dwelling mammal known to science.

» The interbirth period for a female is eight years, making it very difficult for a diminishing population to recover. A female is not ready to give birth until she is 15 years old.

» When an infant is taken for the exotic pet trade, the mother is typically shot.

» The Bornean Orangutan is skilled in the use of tools and uses them on a daily basis – they have even been seen trying to spear fish with branches.

» More than 60 per cent of the orangutan's habitat has been lost in the past 20 years. The Indonesian government tends to overlook this because of the financial benefits of development.

Orangutan ancestors

Fossil records suggest that relatives of the modern orangutans were once more widespread, occurring across mainland South-East Asia and into China. Today they are found only on the islands of Borneo and Sumatra. The Bornean Orangutan and the Sumatran Orangutan are thought to have split about 400,000 years ago. Sumatran Orangutans are more arboreal than their Bornean counterparts, and this is possibly because they face more terrestrial predators such as the Sumatran Tiger.

The Bornean Orangutan is only found on the island of Borneo. Its name in Malay means 'People of the Forest'. There are three subspecies, each occupying a different area of the island. The greatest number are now found in Kalimantan, in the Indonesian part of the island.

The largest orangutan

The Bornean Orangutan is third in size and weight among the great apes, with only the two species of gorilla being larger, but it does qualify as the largest tree-dwelling mammal known to science.

Males weigh an average of 75kg (165lb) and are 1.2–1.4m (3.9–4.6ft) in length. Females are smaller, weighing an average of 38.5kg (85lb) and measuring 1–1.2m (3–3.9ft) in length. They can stretch their arms up to 2m (6.5ft). These arms must support their massive body weight while they swing from tree to tree, high above the ground. Prehensile hands and feet mean that they can grasp branches as they go. They have a coat of wiry red hair and a bare black face. When they come to the ground they walk on all fours, balancing on their clenched fists.

When a male reaches the age of about 20, he may develop flanged protusions on either side of his face. These fleshy pads are unique to the Bornean Orangutan and are totally absent from other primates. They help the male to deliver a long vocalisation during the breeding season, which will attract females from up to 3km (1.9 miles) away.

Bornean Orangutans can expect to live between 35–45 years. In captivity this can increase to 60 years, although many individuals become very overweight.

Mixed diet

The Bornean Orangutan has a very wide and varied diet. About 60 per cent of its intake is fruit, ranging from wild figs to durians, lychees, jackfruit, mangosteens and mangoes. The remainder of its food is made up of young leaves and shoots, seeds, woody lianas, insects, birds' eggs, flowers and honey. They will eat bark, but in smaller quantities than the Sumatran Orangutan. Very rarely they will kill smaller primates such as slow lorises. Occasionally they will eat soil, which gives them the minerals that they need to offset the toxins and acids that they accumulate from their fruit-rich diets. Liquid is obtained from succulent ripe fruit and from water collected in tree hollows.

TOOL USE

The Bornean Orangutan is skilled in the use of tools. They will use them on a daily basis, utilising twigs to inspect water depth, to scratch their back, or to jab a termite mound. Leaves are employed to make umbrellas when it is raining, as a sponge to clean themselves, or as a napkin when eating. Vegetation is used to swat bees or to hold a prickly durian fruit whilst eating. They have even been observed attempting to spear fish with branches. Whilst other primates exhibit tool use, this species shows an extraordinary ability to handle and utilise complicated apparatus.

SLOW BREEDERS

Females tend not to give birth until they are 15 years old, while the interbirth period for a female is eight years. This makes it very difficult for a diminishing population to recover its numbers.

Males and females only socialise during the breeding season, although this can be a complicated affair. An unflanged male will try to attract the attention of any female, managing to mate about 50 per cent of the time. Females prefer to mate with flanged males, who will call to attract their attention. A flanged male will more often mate with a female that is weaning an infant, so that he is sure that she is fertile.

A single infant is born after a gestation period of 234–271 days, and it starts to eat soft food at the age of four months. The youngster will cling to its mother's fur, gripping its fingers around it, and will go everywhere with her for the first three years of its life. At the age of four they tend to start socialising with other young orangutans, although at this age they are never far from their mother's sight, and they will remain close to their mother for 7–11 years.

FOREST DWELLERS

Each orangutan will build a new nest every day, high up in the canopy, bending branches to create a den and adding a top layer if it happens to be raining.

Occasionally, up to a handful of female orangutans may spend time together, but males are solitary. They will only meet females in the breeding season and may elicit menacing responses when encountering other males.

Bornean Orangutan habitat ranges from forested river valleys or floodplains up to more mountainous regions, some of which are 1,500m (4,900ft) above sea-level. These are tropical and subtropical broadleaf forests and the orangutan will move freely around them in search of fruit. The distribution of orangutans has become highly fragmented due to habitat destruction.

POPULATION AND THREATS

Habitat destruction through illegal logging, mining, fire and large-scale expansion of oil palm plantations is a serious dilemma, as are the bushmeat trade and the exotic pet trade.

More than 60 per cent of the orangutan's habitat has been lost in the past 20 years. Orangutan numbers have fallen by 50 per cent in the last 60 years. The north-western subspecies now has only 1,500 individuals living in a small and severely fragmented habitat.

Slash and burn agriculture is used to clear land for crops. On a countrywide level, this decreases habitat for the orangutans and puts their lives in danger. Illegal logging within the protected areas has caused problems on a political level for Indonesia. An infrequent lawsuit in November 2011 saw two men convicted over the killing of 20 orangutans. They told the court that their employer at the palm oil plantation had told them to do it in order to safeguard the crop.

In 1997–98 forest fires killed 8,000 orangutans. These natural forest fires went on for six months and were exacerbated by the drainage of peat-swamp forest for agriculture.

Infant orangutans are caught to sell to the exotic pet trade, and when this happens the mother is typically shot. Although protected by Indonesian law, little seems to be done. Indonesia, as a whole, is a country facing severe poverty. Many orangutans are killed for their meat by starving people.

Although numbers of Bornean Orangutan are greater than those of the Sumatran Orangutan – 54,500 compared to 15,000 – it is feared that the Bornean Orangutan could become extinct within 10–20 years.

CONSERVATION MEASURES

The Indonesian government has set up protected parks, but 50 per cent of orangutans live outside of these. The parks are understaffed and poorly funded, so that their borders are not defended and enforced effectively. Consequently, oil palm companies and logging contractors have moved their operations to within park boundaries. The government tends to overlook this, because of the financial benefits of development.

Selective logging means that orangutans could still get to their fruit trees. Long-term conservation of the forest ecosystem is the ultimate aim.

Outside agencies have been working with the Indonesian government to enforce the law regarding wildlife trade. They work with rescued orangutans to help them rehabilitate before returning to the wild. Ecotourism is also an option being discussed, working with local people to bring economic benefit to the community and thereby amplify the loyalty they feel towards the orangutan.

Flanged male Bornean Orangutan.

Blue Whale

Balaenoptera musculus

KEY FACTS

» The largest animal ever to have lived, measuring up to 29.9m (98ft) in length and with a maximum known weight of 173 tonnes. Its penis is the largest known, at 2.4–3.0m (8–10ft).

» Gives off sounds in the region of 155–188 decibels, which is louder than a jumbo jet engine (140 decibels), and makes them the noisiest animals in existence. This may revise our notion of their solitary social structure, as it may be that they are in continual communication with each other.

» Each whale consumes 40 million krill every day, weighing 3,600kg (7,900lb). Its mouth can hold up to 90 tonnes of water and food, but due to the shape of its throat it cannot swallow anything bigger than a football.

» The global population fell by more than 90 per cent during the 20th century due to whaling. Its numbers have increased to 10,000–15,000 today, located in five distinct groups, but it is still extremely rare.

» Studies indicate that mid-frequency sonar use in the Southern Californian Bight has disrupted the foraging activities of Blue Whales to the point that they even stop feeding altogether.

» Climate change would affect the Blue Whale by disrupting its migratory patterns and impacting on the location and profusion of krill.

Back from the Brink

At up to 29.9m (98ft) in length and with a maximum known weight of 173 tonnes, the Blue Whale is the biggest animal ever to have existed, even bigger than the dinosaurs. It has a huge distribution, being found in every ocean on Earth apart from the Arctic and enclosed seas.

At the start of the 20th century it was relatively numerous, but whalers killed off so many that the species came close to extinction. In 1966, the International Whaling Commission banned hunting of the Blue Whale. By 2002 the population was estimated to be around 5,000–12,000 individuals in five distinct groups, and today this has increased to 10,000–25,000, although it is still extremely rare. The only Blue Whale population showing any real return to health is the one in the eastern North Pacific off California, where from 2014 there were thought to be 2,200 Blue Whales, which is nearly 97 per cent of the pre-whaling population.

Baleen Plates

The Blue Whale is a baleen whale, which means that it does not have teeth. Instead there are about 300 baleen plates which hang from the top jaw. They are individually about 1m (3ft) in length and reach 0.5m (20in) inside of the mouth. Between 70–118 ventral pleats run from the throat along the length of the body. These grooves help to remove water from the mouth during feeding.

A Big Blow

The lung capacity of the Blue Whale is 5,000 litres (1,100 gallons). When it surfaces to breathe it emits a huge column of spray – the 'blow' – which is usually about 9m (30ft) high and sometimes reaches 12m (39ft). When breathing it raises its body further out of the water than other whales, such as the superficially similar Sei or Fin Whales, which makes it easier to spot.

Key Features

The Blue Whale has a lengthy, tapering physique with a U-shaped head and a protruding elevation running from the top of the exterior lip to the blowhole.

It has a comparatively small dorsal fin, which is located three-quarters of the way down its body and is on average 28cm (11in) tall. The flippers are an average of 3–4m (9.8–13.1ft) in length.

The upperparts are bluish with distinct patterns of darker and paler mottling on each individual. The yellow-white on the underside is caused by a build-up of diatoms, which are microscopic marine algae, and this has led to the whale being known by the colloquial name of 'sulphur-bottom whale'.

BIGGEST IN THE WORLD

The Blue Whale's tongue is the biggest in the world, weighing in at a huge 2.7 tonnes. Its mouth can hold up to 90 tonnes of water and food, but due to the shape of its throat it cannot swallow anything bigger than a football. Its heart weights 180kg (400lb).

At birth the calf weighs 2,700kg (6,000lb), which is equal to an adult hippopotamus. The calf will consume 380 litres (84 Imperial gal) of milk daily for seven months. Surprisingly, the Blue Whale brain is comparatively small at 6.92kg (15.26lb), and makes up only 0.007 per cent of its overall mass. However, its penis is the largest known, at 2.4–3.0m (8–10ft) in length.

FEEDING MECHANISM

The Blue Whale can swim at rates of 50kph (31mph) in brief intervals when fraternising with other whales, but 20kph (12mph) is more common and they slow down to 5kph (3.1mph) when feeding. When migrating they swim at depths of 13m (42.5ft) in order to reduce drag from the top of the sea. They have been known to swim to depths of 506m (1,660ft).

A Blue Whale's diet is made up almost entirely of krill, which is a small shrimp-like crustacean. One whale can consume 40 million krill every day, which has a weight of 3,600kg (7,900lb). They need to take in 1.5 million kilocalories (6.3 gigajoules) daily, but during feeding the animal absorbs 90 times more energy than it depletes, giving it fantastic energy efficiency. This comes in useful as their feeding patterns vary throughout the year, with Blue Whales devouring huge quantities of Antarctic krill in the summer, before travelling to the milder but less krill-rich equatorial waters for the winter.

The whale feeds by lunging at the krill, which it takes into its mouth together with a vast amount of water. The water is forced out through the baleen plates by using the tongue and the ventral pouch exerting pressure inside the mouth. The krill, squid, other crustaceans and small fish remain and are consumed by the whale. A whale will dive for 10–20 minutes at depths of 100m (330ft) in order to catch the krill, while it will feed at the surface after dark.

Blue Whales tend to live solitarily or in pairs. They only come together in groups of 50–60 to feed. They differ in social structure from other baleen whales, which often live in sizeable relatively close-knit groups.

BREEDING BEHAVIOUR

The Blue Whale spends the summer in the cool, high latitudes of the Southern Hemisphere where there is an abundance of krill. They migrate towards the Equator in winter.

The mating season begins in autumn and continues until the end of the winter. Research has not been carried out into the species' mating behaviour or breeding grounds, but it is known that a male will follow a female for great lengths of time. If a second male tries to take his place they will race each other, occasionally breaching and causing each other harm.

A female will give birth every two or three years at the beginning of winter, after a gestation period of 10–12 months. The calf is 7m (23ft) long and weighs in the region of 2.5 tonnes. After six months, the calf will be twice its original size and will have weaned from its mother. Mother and calf will remain with each other for a year or so, until the calf is able to follow the whale's migratory sequence by itself. The calf will attain sexual maturity at 5–10 years. Scientists believe that the Blue Whale has a life expectancy of 80 years.

The noisiest animal

The Blue Whale emits sounds at a frequency of between 10–40Hz. The lowest a human can hear is 20Hz. The sounds that a Blue Whale gives off are in the region of 155–188 decibels, which is noisier than a jumbo jet engine (140 decibels), making them the noisiest animals in existence.

Each call can last for 10–30 seconds and in practice can transmit over many thousands of kilometres. This may revise our notion of their solitary social structure, as it may be that they are in continual communication with each other over long distances.

A grotesque slaughter

Blue Whales are big, fast and hard to catch. It was not until 1864 when the Norwegian Svend Foyn attached a specially designed harpoon to a steamboat that whaling began to seriously affect the species. The global population of Blue Whales fell by more than 90 per cent over the course of the 20th century.

The hunting of Blue Whales was halted in 1966 by the International Whaling Committee, with the Soviet Union finally stopping its illegal hunting in the 1970s. At this point 363,000 individuals had been killed in the Southern Hemisphere (mostly in Antarctica), along with 8,200 in the North Pacific and 7,000 in the North Atlantic. The Antarctic, which hosted the biggest population initially, was left with a mere 0.015 per cent of its former number – a scant 360 individuals. This population is now growing at a healthy rate of 7.3 per cent per annum, but there is a lot of ground to make up.

OTHER DANGERS

Strandings of Blue Whales are very rare. The species' sole natural predator is the Orca or Killer Whale, with 25 per cent of all Blue Whales showing signs of an Orca attack. Otherwise the main concerns are all the results of human activity.

These human-induced dangers include collisions with ocean vessels, becoming trapped in fishing nets, chemical and sound pollution, and overfishing of krill. Noise in the ocean, especially sonar, creates havoc with the whale's natural form of communication. Studies indicate that mid-frequency sonar use in the Southern Californian Bight has disrupted the foraging activities of the Blue Whale, even to the point where they stop feeding altogether. One form of chemical pollution is the substance polychlorinated biphenyl (PCB), which builds up in the whale's body.

CLIMATE CHANGE AND HABITAT

Climate change could also be an issue as global warming and correlated acidification of the seas would have a major influence on the availability of krill. Climate change would also effectively redefine the Blue Whale's habitat by shifting existing frontal zones. Frontal zones are particularly beneficial to the whale and they occur at the boundaries between distinct water masses.

Warm water rises from the deep, carrying nutrients. This causes the growth of phytoplankton and creates rich feeding grounds for the whales. Potentially, Blue Whales would have to travel a further 200–500km (125–300 miles) in order to find their key concentrations of prey and enrich themselves for the rest of the year. This would create a longer migration route, and mean that they would have to sustain themselves for longer journeys with probably condensed feeding times.

Another concern regarding climate change is the increase in fresh water in the oceans, due to glaciers and permafrost melting. This extra fresh water could rise to a critical point causing an interference in the thermohaline circulation. The migratory routes of the Blue Whale are dependent on temperature, and the ocean's circulation which transfers warm and cold water currents around the planet would be changed. The increased warming and lower salinity could have a considerable impact on the location and profusion of krill.

INDEX

First published in 2018 by Reed New Holland Publishers Pty Ltd
London • Sydney • Auckland

131–151 Great Titchfield Street, London WIW 5BB, UK
1/66 Gibbes Street, Chatswood, NSW 2067, Australia
5/39 Woodside Avenue, Northcote, Auckland 0627, New Zealand

newhollandpublishers.com

A record of this book is held at the British Library and the National Library of Australia.

ISBN 978 1 92554 627 9

Group Managing Director: Fiona Schultz
Publisher and Project Editor: Simon Papps
Designer: Sara Lindberg
Production Director: James Mills-Hicks
Printed in China by Easy Fame (Hong Kong) Limited

Image credits as follows: Shutterstock.com (individual photographer names in brackets): pages 4, 184 (Vaclav Sebek); 6 (Radu Razvan); 11 (Miki Studio); 12 (Louis W); 18–19 (Tristan Tan); 20 (Dirk Ercken); 25 (Ivan Kuzmin); 26–27 (Vladimir Wrangel); 29 (Peter Vrabel); 32–33 (Dean Bertoncelj); 34 (Thanatham Piriyakarnjanakul); 40-41 (vanchai); 42–43 (Nagel Photography); 50 (Peter Gilson); 53, 56–57 (Don Mammoser); 58 (Naas Rautenbach); 64, 69 (Ryan M. Bolton); 70 (Andrey Armyagov); 72 (KorradolYamsatthm); 75 (orlandin); 76–77 (stephan kerkhofs); 78 (ACEgan); 83 (IrinaK); 84–85 (amskad); 86 (kojihirano); 88 (Christopher Gardiner); 92 (Infiniumguy); 93 (rlsmithtx); 94 (Edwin Verin); 99 (Stephane Bidouze); 101 (Casper Simon); 102 (Michal Pesata); 104 (MrPhotoMania); 108, 110, 114–115 (Wang LiQiang); 116, 119 (2630ben); 123 (Positive Snapshot); 124 (Stacey Ann Alberts); 126 (Johan Swanepoel); 129 (Cathy Withers-Clarke); 132, 136–137, 140 (Gudkov Andrey); 139 (Vladislav T. Jirousek); 142 (Jean-Edouard Rozey); 147 (Joanna Wu); 150 (Rich Carey); 152 (Foto Mous);157 (Kathryn Carroll); 158 (HelloRF Zcool); 165 (Marisa Estivill); 166, front cover (Anne-Marie B); 171 (Sukpaiboonwat); 173 (dptro); 174 (Onyx9); 177 (Marian Galovic); 181 (Simon Eeman); 182–183 (Erwin F); 190 (R.M. Nunes); 192, 197 (Sergey Uryadnikov); 198–199 (Andrew Sutton); 203 (Powell's Point); and 205 (Joe Morris 917).

10 9 8 7 6 5 4 3 2 1

Keep up with New Holland Publishers on Facebook
www.facebook.com/NewHollandPublishers